# WHO ATE LUNCH WITH ABRAHAM?

A study of the appearances of God in the form
of a Man in the Hebrew Scriptures

By
ASHER INTRATER

Intermedia Publishing Group

# WHO ATE LUNCH WITH ABRAHAM?

Published by:
Intermedia Publishing Group, Inc.
P.O. Box 2825
Peoria, Arizona 85380
www.intermediapub.com

ISBN 978-1-935906-66-7

All translations in this book are the author's. Translations from the Hebrew Scriptures are direct from the original. Translations of the New Covenant are a reconstruction adapted from the Modern Hebrew translation (The Bible Society in Israel). Hebrew text translations are occasionally compared to the New King James version, Nelson Publishers, as well.

# WHO ATE LUNCH WITH WITH ABRAHAM?

A study of the appearances of God in the form
of a Man in the Hebrew Scriptures

# TABLE OF CONTENTS

Foreword: Can You See God?                                    i

Part One: The Patriarchs
    Chapter One: Who Ate Lunch with Abraham?          1
    Chapter Two: Who Kicked Jacob in the Leg?         9
    Chapter Three: Why was Yeshua Circumcised?        15

Part Two: The Exodus
    Chapter Four: The Angel of Yehovah                27
    Chapter Five: Who Wrote the Ten Commandments?     35
    Chapter Six: Yeshua and the Moral Law             45

Part Three: The Conquest
    Chapter Seven: The Commander-in-Chief             57
    Chapter Eight: Who Fought the Battle of Jericho?  65
    Chapter Nine: Possessing the Land                 73

Part Four: The Prophets
    Chapter Ten: Who Is Sitting in the Chair?         87
    Chapter Eleven: My Eyes Have Seen the King        97
    Chapter Twelve: The Son of Man                    107

Part Five: The Revelation
    Chapter Thirteen: Who Is the Man on Fire?         117
    Chapter Fourteen: John's Divine Revelation        123

Summary: The Mystery Man                                      131

Appendices

   1. Reference List of Divine Appearances
      in the Hebrew Scriptures 143

   2. The Divine Angel, by Solomon Intrater 146

   3. Yehovah and Yahweh 149

   4. Yehovah and Yeshua 153

   5. Keeping the Sabbath 155

   6. Ladder of Gospel and Law 158

   7. Restoration of All Things 161

   8. Heaven and Earth 164

   9. Before the Foundation 168

  10. Human and Glorified Appearances 170

  11. Divine and Davidic 172

  12. Scholarly Support, by Dan Juster 174

About the Author 177

# Can You See God?

There is a figure who appears throughout the Law and the Prophets. He is sometimes referred to as the Angel of the Lord, sometimes as God Himself, sometimes as "One like the Son of Man," and often with no name at all. Understanding who this figure is represents a challenge to our most fundamental concepts about God and the Messiah.

Seeing the connection between the Angel of the Lord in the Tanakh (Hebrew Scriptures) and the figure of Yeshua (Jesus) in the New Covenant is challenging to both the Christian and Jewish world views. This book is meant to be equally challenging to both sides, in a balanced way, forming a bridge to both Jewish and Christian understanding.

The primary purpose of this book is to describe the appearances of God and the nature of the Messiah as found in the Scriptures. We desire that truth above all others.

This book also has three secondary purposes:

1. Deepening the Jewish roots of the Christian faith
2. Describing who Yeshua is from the Hebrew Scriptures
3. Demonstrating the consistency of the Bible from beginning to end

## Jewish Roots

I grew up in a liberal Jewish home and attended a conservative synagogue in my youth. During my college years, I found myself on a search for spiritual truth. My personal search and my studies in psychology, philosophy and ancient literatures at Harvard did not lead me to anything that satisfied my soul.

I tried all kinds of spiritual experiences and experiments. The one thing that I was not willing to consider was Jesus. However, in an effort to be consistent in my search for truth, I realized that I had to read the gospels at least one time (even though I was convinced beforehand that there would be nothing very good in them).

The first time I read the gospels in the winter of 1977-78, I was surprised at how positive they were. The person of Yeshua, His life and His teachings, inspired both love and awe. It was difficult not to "fall in love" with that inspiring figure.

The second time I read the gospels in the summer of 1978, I had a second surprise. I realized how "Jewish" the book was. Everyone in it was Jewish, including Yeshua Himself and all the disciples. More than that, the entire world view about the kingdom of God was taken from the Hebrew Prophets.

Because of the first surprise, I dedicated my life to be a follower of Yeshua in 1978. Because of the second surprise, I found myself as part of what is popularly called "Messianic Judaism." At that point, I continued studies, not only in the Bible, but also in Christian literature and in Rabbinic writings. (As part of those studies, I completed in the early 1980s two masters' degrees, one in Jewish Studies from Baltimore Hebrew University, and one in theology from Messiah Biblical Institute.)

There are many issues concerning the Jewish roots of Christianity. One of the most challenging is the figure of the Angel of the Lord in the Torah (Law) and Prophets. This book hopes to deal with those issues.

### Yeshua in the Tanakh

A fascinating element of the New Covenant is its love for all mankind, and particularly for the Jewish people. There is no room for any racism at all, yet the continuing role of Israel as a chosen nation is confirmed over and over again (for example, **Rom. 9-11**). Yeshua weeps over Jerusalem (**Luke 19:41-44**), and Saul (the apostle Paul) said he would be willing to die for the Jews (**Rom. 9:1-4**).

In my new found faith in Yeshua, I found a new love for my own people as well. I was stirred to share with my family about God's grace and about eternal life. Since many Jewish people accept the authority of the Tanakh but not the New Covenant, it is often necessary to explain God's plan of salvation in Yeshua from the Tanakh alone. (The early apostles shared Yeshua from the Tanakh alone, since they were still in the process of writing the New Covenant.)

There are many wonderful prophecies about the Messiah in the Tanakh. The apostles often started with those prophecies—for example, in **Acts 8** Philip shares with the Ethiopian eunuch from **Isaiah 53**. In God's particular plan for my life, I ended up sharing the good news of salvation in Hebrew here in Israel, often with Orthodox Jews. I found that sharing the prophecies alone was not enough. The problem is that even if the prophecies are crystal clear, one whose heart is not open can just say that he doesn't agree with our interpretation.

Through much study and prayer (along with a lot of arguments, conflicts and personal experience), I began to see another way: not just **prophecies about** the Messiah but actual **appearances of** the Messiah in the form of the Angel of the Lord. The connection between the Angel of the Lord and Yeshua the Messiah is truly enlightening. It is that dynamic revelation that I hope to share in this book.

## Consistency of Scriptures

Many years ago, my friend Dan Juster shared with me the philosophical principle that truth must be consistent within itself. If a teaching contradicts itself, it cannot be true. This principle applies to philosophy, theology, biblical interpretation and all logical thinking.

Yeshua verified this when He said that He came not to nullify or contradict anything that was written in the Law and the Prophets, but to fulfill them (**Matt. 5:17-18**). The apostle Saul repeated this principle over and over again (**Acts 24:14; 26:22; 28:23**).

I believe the Bible to be true and trustworthy. As such, it must be internally consistent from Genesis through to Revelation. Genesis starts with the creation of heaven and earth; Revelation ends with the creation of the new heavens and new earth. What God intended in the beginning is brought to completion at the end. [The Rabbis say, סוף מעשה במחשבה תחילה—"What is final in deed is first in the thought." (Shabbat hymn לכה דודי by R. Shlomo Halevy Alkabets, Sixteenth Century.)]

The kingdom of God proceeds through various stages from a tiny seed until a mighty tree that fills the whole earth (**Matt. 13:31-32; Mark 4:26-28**). There are different stages, but the development is consistent from beginning to end.

Unfortunately, because of the divisive history between Christianity and Judaism, rabbis and priests alike have built thick walls of theology which reinforce an artificial separation between the first stage of God's plan as revealed to Israel and the second stage as revealed to the Church. Two thousand years of disagreement between Israel and the Church have created a barrier to understanding the consistency of Scriptures. One of the keys to breaking down that barrier is the connection between the Angel of the Lord and Yeshua the Messiah.

The Scriptures are consistent because the nature of God is consistent. That consistency is also true of the nature of the Messiah. Yeshua is the same in the past, the present and the future (**Heb. 13:8**). Yeshua is the common thread that links the Scriptures together. The eternal nature of the Messiah demonstrates the consistency of the Scriptures. By showing the central role of the Angel of the Lord in the Law and the Prophets, it is my hope that this book will help affirm the consistency of Scriptures from the Law of Moses through to the Revelation of John.

I hope you enjoy it and find these ideas as enlightening as I did.

*Asher Intrater*

# PART ONE

# The Patriarchs

---

*In this section, we examine the appearances of God to Abraham and the patriarchs in the book of Genesis.*

*In this period we discover the appearance of a Divine Messenger who comes in the form of a man, a God-Man. We will compare the appearances of that God-Man to the figure of Yeshua (Jesus) in the New Covenant.*

*We will also consider how those appearances affect our understanding of Jewish calling and God's covenants with Israel.*

# CHAPTER ONE
## Who Ate Lunch with Abraham?

One of the popular beliefs of Judaism is that it is impossible to see God. From the thirteen foundational principles of the faith by Rabbi Moshe Ben Maimon (1135-1204), the prayer hymn "Yigdal," and the creed "Ani Maamin," we find the words:

אֵין לוֹ דְּמוּת הַגּוּף וְאֵינוֹ גּוּף

"God has no form of body and has no body."

This understanding is derived from **Deuteronomy 4:12:**

**And the Lord spoke to you out of the midst of the fire. You heard the sound of the words, but saw no form; you only heard a voice.**

וַיְדַבֵּר יְהֹוָה אֲלֵיכֶם מִתּוֹךְ הָאֵשׁ קוֹל דְּבָרִים אַתֶּם שֹׁמְעִים וּתְמוּנָה אֵינְכֶם רֹאִים זוּלָתִי קוֹל

However, this verse does not say that God has no form. It says that the people at Sinai did not see any form. The verse in context is not making a statement about the visibility of God. It is a warning against the making of graven images and worshiping idols **(vv. 15-24)**.

The belief that it is impossible to see God is partially true and partially not true. The invisibility of God is also reiterated in the New Covenant:

| | |
|---|---|
| **John 1:18** | **No one has seen God at any time** |
| **John 5:37** | **You have not... seen His form** |
| **John 6:46** | **Not that anyone has seen the Father** |
| **Colossians 1:15** | **He is the image of the invisible God** |
| **1 Timothy 1:17** | **To the King eternal, immortal, invisible** |
| **1 Timothy 6:16** | **Whom no man has seen or can see** |
| **1 John 4:12** | **No one has seen God at any time** |
| **1 John 4:20** | **...how can he love God whom he has not seen?** |

With all these verses, it is easy to understand why people think that it is impossible to see God. However, when taken in context a different picture arises. The fact that people do not normally see God does not mean that He is un-seeable. Rather, because of our fallen condition, we are not able to see Him. If we were to see God in the fullness of His power, it would kill us (**Exod. 33:20**). We will deal with this difference at length in part two.

On the one hand it is impossible to see God. On the other hand, our patriarchs and prophets did see "Someone" from time to time. Abraham saw this "Someone" on several occasions:

**Genesis 12:7—Then YHVH appeared to Abram...**

וַיֵּרָא יְהוָה אֶל־אַבְרָם

**Genesis 15:1—And the word—YHVH came to Abram in a vision...**

הָיָה דְבַר־יְהוָה אֶל־אַבְרָם בַּמַּחֲזֶה

**Genesis 17:1—And YHVH appeared to Abram...**

וַיֵּרָא יְהוָה אֶל־אַבְרָם

**Genesis 18:1—Then YHVH appeared to him at the oaks of Mamre...**

וַיֵּרָא אֵלָיו יְהוָה בְּאֵלֹנֵי מַמְרֵא

In the verses above the word *appeared* in Hebrew is the passive form of the verb *to see*. It clearly means that Abraham saw something, and could also be translated as "was seen by Abraham."

On the first three occasions we have no description of whom or what Abraham saw. However, in chapter 18, the description is detailed and specific. Scholars and rabbinic commentators go to great lengths to explain that this chapter cannot be taken in a literal or plain sense meaning (פשט). Yet, the text is explicit and quite "physical" in the detail of its descriptions.

The staggering and inescapable truth is that YHVH Himself comes to visit Abraham in the form of a human being. He eats lunch with him, and they discuss together a number of important issues, from the upcoming pregnancy of Sarah to the impending destruction of Sodom. (Please take a few moments to read the entire chapter of Genesis 18 and then follow along in your Bible as we analyze it.)

[Note: From this point on we will use the term "Yehovah" to translate the name YHVH. It is imperative for this study to know when that name is being used in the original text, so we can not translate the name by the generic, "Lord" or "LORD." For a discussion on the decision and preference to use the name Yehovah, see Appendix #3, "Yehovah or Yahweh." Writing Yehovah instead of YHVH also makes the text a little more readable, even though there are no vowel points in the original Hebrew.]

**Genesis 18:1-2**

**Then Yehovah appeared to him at the oaks of Mamre, as he was sitting at the tent opening in the heat of the day. So he lifted his eyes and saw, and behold three men were standing by him; and when he saw them, he ran from the tent opening to meet them, and bowed himself down to the ground.**

וַיֵּרָא אֵלָיו יְהוָה בְּאֵלֹנֵי מַמְרֵא וְהוּא יֹשֵׁב פֶּתַח־הָאֹהֶל כְּחֹם הַיּוֹם: וַיִּשָּׂא עֵינָיו וַיַּרְא וְהִנֵּה שְׁלֹשָׁה אֲנָשִׁים נִצָּבִים עָלָיו וַיַּרְא וַיָּרָץ לִקְרָאתָם מִפֶּתַח הָאֹהֶל וַיִּשְׁתַּחוּ אָרְצָה

Abraham saw **"three men"** coming to visit him. Who are these three men? One of the three was called Yehovah; the other two were angels.

**Genesis 19:1—Then the two angels came to Sodom...**

וַיָּבֹאוּ שְׁנֵי הַמַּלְאָכִים סְדֹמָה

These were not any two angels, but *the* two angels. They were the same two angels who were with Yehovah and Abraham. The three visitors that Abraham saw were 1) Yehovah in the bodily form of a man, and 2) two angels. All three are called "men."

Two angels and the Yehovah-Man came to visit Abraham in the heat of the day. In exquisite Bedouin hospitality, Abraham leaps to his feet and runs to welcome them. But this is not mere hospitality. One reason that Abraham ran to them is that he recognized this Yehovah-Man. He had already seen Him several times before.

Abraham runs to Him, bows down and calls Him Lord. The word here for bow down is וישתחו, which may be translated as either "bow down" or "worship." It is the primary Hebraic word for "worship." The word for Lord here is אדוני, Adonai, which is the plural form of Lord, most often used in reference to the name Yehovah.

Throughout Genesis chapter 18, there is not one indication that Abraham does not recognize and realize with whom he is speaking. He treats Him as Yehovah, and as "Someone" he already knows. The three figures of the group are called "men" three times: in verse 2, verse 16 and verse 22. The special One in the group is called Yehovah four times: verse 1 (above), verse 17, verse 22, and verse 33.

**Genesis 18:16-17**

**Then the men arose from there and looked toward Sodom, and Abraham was walking with them to send them on the way. And Yehovah said, "Shall I cover up from Abraham that which I am doing?"**

וַיָּקֻמוּ מִשָּׁם הָאֲנָשִׁים וַיַּשְׁקִפוּ עַל־פְּנֵי סְדֹם וְאַבְרָהָם
הֹלֵךְ עִמָּם לְשַׁלְּחָם: וַיהוָה אָמָר הַמְכַסֶּה אֲנִי מֵאַבְרָהָם
אֲשֶׁר אֲנִי עֹשֶׂה:

After they finish eating lunch and talking about Isaac's birth, the three "men" get up to leave. The two angels go on to do their work in Sodom. The Yehovah-Man stays to talk a little more with Abraham alone.

**Genesis 18:22**

**Then the men turned away from there and went toward Sodom, but Abraham still stood before Yehovah.**

וַיִּפְנוּ מִשָּׁם הָאֲנָשִׁים וַיֵּלְכוּ סְדֹמָה וְאַבְרָהָם עוֹדֶנּוּ עֹמֵד לִפְנֵי יְהוָה:

Abraham and Yehovah discuss issues of judgment and grace concerning Sodom. By the time they finish talking, the two angels are well on their way to arrive in Sodom. At the end of the conversation, the Yehovah-Man leaves, presumably to go back to heaven.

**Genesis 18:33-19:1a**

**So Yehovah left when He finished speaking to Abraham, and Abraham returned to his place. Now the two angels came to Sodom.**

וַיֵּלֶךְ יְהוָה כַּאֲשֶׁר כִּלָּה לְדַבֵּר אֶל־אַבְרָהָם וְאַבְרָהָם שָׁב לִמְקֹמוֹ: וַיָּבֹאוּ שְׁנֵי הַמַּלְאָכִים סְדֹמָה

The two angels go on to rescue Lot and destroy Sodom. The whole encounter of Abraham with Yehovah in Genesis 18 is described in realistic detail. The weather is hot. They eat a full meal, including meat and milk together. The destruction of Sodom is tangible. This is not portrayed as a dream or vision, but as an actual historical event.

One may or may not believe that the Bible is true. However, it is unquestionable that the biblical text considers this event to have taken place literally. In this description, we have an astonishing biblical claim: Yehovah is seen, heard and touched. Yehovah has come to visit man in a human form.

The ultimate stumbling block for a religious Jew to believe in Yeshua is the claim of Yeshua's being divine, not of His being the Messiah. The orthodox Jewish *Chabad* movement has made claims in recent years that their deceased head rabbi, Rebbe Schneerson, had divine attributes. However, their view is somewhat less than the level of the New Covenant claim of Yeshua's divinity.

The bottom-line issue is our understanding of the nature of God. The idea that God could take on the form of a man, a bodily form, and come to visit mankind seems non-monotheistic, let alone non-

Jewish. The root problem is not the interpretation of Messianic prophecies but the essence of who the Messiah is. To think of "God becoming incarnate" seems abhorrent, almost blasphemous.

Yet here we have it. Our father Abraham meets with God manifest in human bodily form. If God appeared to Abraham in human form, then the foundational objection to the divinity of Yeshua disappears. Genesis 18 is a more radical God-incarnate passage than any chapter in the entire New Covenant.

One may reasonably argue that he does not see the figure in Genesis 18 as Yeshua. However, it cannot be reasonably argued that the Genesis 18 text does not describe an appearance of Yehovah in human bodily form. That appearance of God in a human form to Abraham removes the most fundamental reason in Jewish thinking for not believing in Yeshua.

In the New Covenant, John chapter 8 does specifically make the claim that the One who visited Abraham was Yeshua. In a heated discussion with some religious leaders, the issue of Abraham came up. Yeshua replied:

**John 8:56-59**

**Your father Abraham rejoiced to see My day, and indeed saw, and rejoiced. They said to Him, "You are not yet fifty years old, and you have seen Abraham?" Yeshua responded to them, "Truly, truly I say to you, before Abraham was, I am." For this they picked up stones to throw at Him.**

Yeshua made several shocking statements here. One could understand why the religious leaders would be offended and tempted to stone Him. Yeshua said He was alive before the time of Abraham. He said that Abraham rejoiced to see His day. Yeshua didn't mean that Abraham rejoiced in a vision or rejoiced in seeing a date on the calendar. Abraham rejoiced to see Yeshua on the day He visited him in Genesis 18. Many translations incorrectly insert in verse 56 the word "it." Abraham didn't rejoice to see "it." He rejoiced to see Him.

This can readily be seen by the response of the religious leaders when they said, "You have seen Abraham?" It was clear that they understood that Yeshua claimed that He and Abraham met and saw one another.

Yeshua stated here that He existed before Abraham. He also said, "Before Abraham was, I am." That is a reference to the name Yehovah. The man in Genesis 18 is referred to four times as Yehovah. The name Yehovah and the name "I AM THAT I AM" are the same name (**Exod. 3:14-15**). What could be the possible conclusion here other than that Yeshua is directly claiming to be the Yehovah-I AM Man who had lunch with Abraham in Genesis 18?

Perhaps Yeshua was mentally unstable. But that is what He said. And that is how the religious leaders understood what He said. That is what so infuriated them to the point of wanting to kill Him. This was not a very "seeker-sensitive" approach. Yeshua left them only three options: To think He was insane, to kill Him for being a blasphemer, or to believe that He was the Yehovah-Man that visited Abraham.

For the religious leaders of the first century, deciding between Yeshua's insanity or His divinity was not a very easy choice. We Jewish people should desire to follow in the footsteps of Abraham. We should believe in the same God he did. To the extent that God appeared to Abraham as a man is the same degree to which we should believe that God can become a man; not more and not less. Our faith is consistent with that of our forefathers.

According to both the Torah and the New Covenant, there is an aspect of God which we cannot see. And there is another aspect of God who appears in the bodily form of a human being. This dual aspect of not being able to see God, yet seeing God manifested in a human-like form is what John described this way:

**John 1:18—No man has seen God at any time. The only begotten Son, who is in the bosom of the Father, He has made Him known.**

The God we cannot see is the one Yeshua referred to as "our Father in heaven." The one we can see and touch in a bodily form is referred to by several names, including the Word of God, the

Angel of Yehovah, the Son of Man, and the Son of God. (We will discuss those references in detail in the coming chapters.) The claim of the New Covenant is that Yeshua is that person.

One can see a parallel between Abraham eating lunch with the Yehovah-Man in Genesis 18 and Yeshua eating with His disciples at the last supper and on the shores of Galilee. Think of the dynamic: intimate yet awesome; mystic yet earthly; divine yet human—God and man having fellowship over a covenant meal. Think of the smell and taste of the food, of the perspiration in the hot Middle East sun. Think of the manly conversations about justice, family, and the coming Messianic kingdom. They experienced eternal revelation in the midst of a most temporal situation.

You and I are invited into that same covenantal friendship that Abraham had, with the same Yehovah-Man that he knew.

# CHAPTER TWO
## *Who Kicked Jacob in the Leg?*

The encounters that Abraham had with this Yehovah-Man were the most important experiences of his life. Doubtless he told everyone around him about them. That would have included his wife, children, maidservants, menservants and neighbors.

His wife's maid servant Hagar also had an encounter with this special person. In her case, He was referred to as the Angel of Yehovah. The Angel of Yehovah met her as she was running away from Sarah. He promised to bless her and her children through Ishmael.

**Genesis 16:7—Now the Angel of Yehovah found her by the spring of water in the desert.**

וַיִּמְצָאָהּ מַלְאַךְ יְהֹוָה עַל־עֵין הַמַּיִם בַּמִּדְבָּר

This was no ordinary angel. He is called the Angel of Yehovah as well in verses 9, 10 and 11. However, in verse 13, this angel is referred to simply by the name Yehovah.

**Genesis 16:13—Then she called the name of Yehovah who spoke to her, "You are God who sees me."**

וַתִּקְרָא שֵׁם־יְהֹוָה הַדֹּבֵר אֵלֶיהָ אַתָּה אֵל רֳאִי

There are many angels, and they often appear to the sons of men. Yet, there is another figure, called the Angel of Yehovah. He is different. He speaks as God in the first person, and He is called by the name Yehovah. In this passage as well, the Angel of Yehovah speaks to her as if He were God, and is called by the name Yehovah. (We will deal extensively with the Angel of the Lord figure in part two.)

This same angel also appeared to Abraham at the time of the sacrifice of Isaac. This was no ordinary angel. Just as Abraham raises the knife, we read:

**Genesis 22:11—But the Angel of Yehovah called unto him from the heavens.**

וַיִּקְרָא אֵלָיו מַלְאַךְ יְהֹוָה מִן־הַשָּׁמַיִם

The angel then begins to speak to him as God in the first person.

**Genesis 22:12—For now I know that you fear God, since you have not withheld your son, your only son, from Me.**

כִּי עַתָּה יָדַעְתִּי כִּי־יְרֵא אֱלֹהִים אַתָּה וְלֹא חָשַׂכְתָּ
אֶת־בִּנְךָ אֶת־יְחִידְךָ מִמֶּנִּי׃

**Genesis 22:16—And said, "I have sworn by Myself," says Yehovah…**

וַיֹּאמֶר בִּי נִשְׁבַּעְתִּי נְאֻם־יְהֹוָה

**Genesis 22:17—Blessing I will bless you and multiplying I will multiply your seed…**

כִּי־בָרֵךְ אֲבָרֶכְךָ וְהַרְבָּה אַרְבֶּה אֶת־זַרְעֲךָ

It would not be reasonable for a normal angel to speak this way in the first person in referring to himself as God.

In fact, the patriarchs named the place Mount Moriah, which means literally: "Mountain Yehovah Appears."

**Genesis 22:14—On the mountain Yehovah will appear.**

יֵאָמֵר הַיּוֹם בְּהַר יְהֹוָה יֵרָאֶה

The appearance of this Angel was regarded by them as an appearance of Yehovah. In this case the Angel is present at the time of Abraham offering Isaac. The "binding" of Isaac is a foundational image of all the future Temple sacrifices, and those sacrifices were seen in the light of the "sacrifice" of Isaac. Both the Temple sacrifice and Isaac's binding were symbolic of the future sacrifice of the Messiah. Isaac is an image of the Messiah. The Angel was present at that symbolic sacrifice. In effect, the Angel is witnessing the symbolic portrayal of His own sacrifice, due to take place almost 2,000 years in the future.

The Bible records a second and a third time that Yehovah appeared unto Isaac.

**Genesis 26:2—Then Yehovah appeared unto him...**

וַיֵּרָא אֵלָיו יְהֹוָה

**Genesis 26:24—And Yehovah appeared unto him on that night...**

וַיֵּרָא אֵלָיו יְהֹוָה בַּלַּיְלָה הַהוּא

In all three of these appearances, the verb root and form in Hebrew are the same as in the appearances of Yehovah unto Abraham.

Awareness of this divine visitor was passed on from Abraham through Isaac to Abraham's grandson Jacob. Jacob had several visitations of this God-in-the-form-of-a-Man. In the first encounter, Jacob is running away from his brother Esau. That night he has a dream in which he sees a ladder standing between heaven and earth with angels ascending and descending.

All those were normal angels. But, at the top of the ladder he sees another figure.

**Genesis 28:13—And behold, Yehovah stood on top of it and said, "I am Yehovah the God of Abraham your father and the God of Isaac."**

וְהִנֵּה יְהֹוָה נִצָּב עָלָיו וַיֹּאמַר אֲנִי יְהֹוָה אֱלֹהֵי אַבְרָהָם אָבִיךָ וֵאלֹהֵי יִצְחָק

After Jacob has this vision, he sets up a pillar of rocks, anoints it with oil and makes a vow unto the Lord. He then names the place Beth El, the house of God.

In this chapter, it is not written explicitly that Yehovah's appearance was in the form of a man. However, we need to ask ourselves just what was it that Jacob saw standing on a ladder. The implication is that it was a human-like form, since a ladder is made in form for humans.

The Bible clarifies who this was in Jacob's ladder dream when Yehovah appears to him the second time. The second time takes place when Jacob is being mistreated by his uncle Laban, and Jacob has the dream about the spotted male sheep mounting the female sheep. Here the divine visitor returns in the name "Angel of Yehovah." Jacob is recounting the dream to his wives:

**Genesis 31:11—Then the Angel of God spoke to me in the dream, "Jacob." And I said, "Here I am."**

וַיֹּאמֶר אֵלַי מַלְאַךְ הָאֱלֹהִים בַּחֲלוֹם יַעֲקֹב וָאֹמַר הִנֵּנִי:

One might think that in the first appearance to Jacob at the ladder, God did not appear in a human form. One might also think that in this second appearance, Jacob saw just an ordinary angel. However, this "angel" then says to Jacob something very out of the ordinary.

**Genesis 31:13—I am the God of Beth El, where you anointed the pillar, where you made a vow to Me.**

אָנֹכִי הָאֵל בֵּית־אֵל אֲשֶׁר מָשַׁחְתָּ שָּׁם מַצֵּבָה אֲשֶׁר נָדַרְתָּ
לִי שָׁם נֶדֶר

The implications of this statement are shocking. The Angel of Yehovah appears unto Jacob. He is clearly a messenger, a "sent one." Then this Angel says, "I am God. I am the God of Abraham and Isaac. I am the one you saw in the first vision." Here is an angel declaring himself to be God.

Let us summarize: In the first appearance (**Gen. 28**), Yehovah God appears. In the second appearance (**Gen. 31**), an angel appears. This angel states forthrightly that he is the Yehovah God that appeared in the first appearance. He is not *an* angel, but *the* Angel. Yehovah God turns out to be the Angel; and the Angel turns out to be Yehovah God. They are one and the same.

This figure, this God-Man-Angel, is the one that Abraham, Isaac and Jacob called their God. Modern textual criticism might refer to this description as an anachronism or anthropomorphism. However, those kinds of academic terms did not exist in Abraham's, Isaac's, or Jacob's day. What is written in the Bible reflects what they knew of God, what they experienced of God, and what they believed about God. It may sound primitive to some today, but to them it was real.

The third divine visitation to Jacob is even more challenging. Here Jacob is returning from exile and is frightened at the prospect of meeting his brother Esau again, from whom he fled some twenty years previously. Jacob sends his wife and children on ahead of him, and stays alone at night by the river Yabok.

**Genesis 32:24—Then Jacob was left alone, and a man wrestled with him until the rise of the dawn.**

וַיִּוָּתֵר יַעֲקֹב לְבַדּוֹ וַיֵּאָבֵק אִישׁ עִמּוֹ עַד עֲלוֹת הַשָּׁחַר:

This time the appearance was not in a dream. Someone shows up in the middle of the night and starts wrestling with Jacob. Neither of them seems to be winning, so the mystery man gives Jacob a punch in the back of the thigh (what we might call a "pulled hamstring" today). Jacob refuses to let go despite the pain, and demands for this man to bless him.

If Jacob is asking the mystery man to bless him, he probably has already has figured out who it is. The man then changes Jacob's name to Israel—from "heal-grabber" to "prince of God." Jacob then asks the man to tell him His name, but the request is not granted. Jacob, now Israel, calls the name of the place Peniel, the face of God.

**Genesis 32:30—So Jacob called the name of the place Peniel: "For I have seen God face to face, and my life is preserved."**

וַיִּקְרָא יַעֲקֹב שֵׁם הַמָּקוֹם פְּנִיאֵל כִּי־רָאִיתִי אֱלֹהִים
פָּנִים אֶל־פָּנִים וַתִּנָּצֵל נַפְשִׁי:

In **verse 25** our mystery figure is called a man; in **verse 31** He is called God. So is He God or is He man? Or is He a God-Man? The next morning Jacob finds he is still limping. Why did God kick him in the leg? The answer is to assure Jacob that this was no dream; this was the real thing. Jacob was a spiritual dreamer. Whenever he was tempted to think that encounter was just a dream or an unreal, mystical experience, a pain shot through the back of his thigh— just to remind him how real it was.

This encounter was with a man who was also God. It was God who came in the form of a man. It happened in a physical body. (If you don't believe that, "Watch out for your hamstring!") Jacob and his whole family were so shocked by the experience that they didn't eat meat from the back of the thigh for generations to come.

A few years later, God tells Jacob to go back to Beth El. There God appears to him a <u>fourth</u> time (**Gen. 35:9-13**). God reviews with Jacob the covenant promises that were previously made at Beth El. (It is possible that this is not an additional visitation, but a review of what happened before. Yet, there are new details and insights which point to it being a new appearance. In either case, the point is the same.)

Perhaps there is still some question whether the man at Peniel was God. However, look what is written in this review of the Peniel encounter. The divine visitor reiterates the covenant promises; He reminds him of the blessing and of how He changed his name to Israel. This is clearly the same "Person" speaking.

**Genesis 35:9, 11—Then God appeared to Jacob again... Also God said to him, "I am God Almighty (*El Shaddai*)."**

וַיֵּרָא אֱלֹהִים אֶל־יַעֲקֹב עוֹד... וַיֹּאמֶר לוֹ אֱלֹהִים אֲנִי אֵל שַׁדָּי

El Shaddai God says, "I am the Man who wrestled with you at Peniel." And in reverse, the Man who wrestled with Jacob at Peniel says, "I am El Shaddai." El Shaddai, the great provider God, who makes covenant and blesses families and finances, appeared many times to our forefathers in the form of a man. This El Shaddai is the same Man who wrestled with Jacob that night at Peniel. He claimed to be both Man and God.

Our forefathers knew El Shaddai in the form of a God-Man-Angel. However, His exact identity was somewhat of a mystery to them. In later years, He was to be revealed as Messiah. As our forefathers made covenant with El Shaddai, so do we make new covenant with Yeshua. He was the God-Man our forefathers believed in. He is the Messiah.

# CHAPTER THREE
## *Why was Yeshua Circumcised?*

El Shaddai was the God of Abraham, Isaac and Jacob. He appeared to our forefathers as a Man and as an Angel. Although this God-Man-Angel was often referred to as Yehovah, He did not reveal His personal name (**Gen. 32:30**), because His personal name was not to be revealed until a future time. That time would come when this God-Man-Angel would be born into this world as Messiah.

The revelation that the God-Man-Angel of the Tanakh would be born into this earth as a man is astonishing. It is an epiphany, a manifestation of God to mankind. This is what John claimed when he said that, "**The Word became flesh and dwelled among us**" (**John 1:14**). It is also what Saul (Paul) meant when he said, "**Great is the mystery of godliness: God was manifested in the flesh**" (**1 Tim. 3:16**).

The importance of the birth of Yeshua is well known in Christian circles, and is known as the "incarnation." In this chapter I would like to deal with a specific aspect of Yeshua's birth that is probably overlooked by most Christians and Jews alike—Yeshua's circumcision. Yeshua was not only born, He was circumcised. He not only came into this world, He was circumcised when He got here.

The surgical procedure of the circumcision is less significant. However, the covenant commitment that is indicated by that procedure is enormous. Circumcision is to the Jewish people what a marriage ring is to a wedding. It is a sign that the covenant has been cut.

The God-Man-Angel cut covenant with the patriarchs. By covenant He chose us as a nation and gave us the land of Israel. It was as if He said to the patriarchs, "I can't tell you My name now. My name is connected to the covenant. One day I will be born into this earth and cut the covenant by being circumcised Myself. At that time, My mysterious name will be revealed." Yeshua cut covenant with the Jewish people when He was circumcised in the flesh; He cut covenant with all mankind when He was crucified in the flesh.

The Christ-Messiah and the God-Man-Angel are one and the same. He did not have a private name in the time of the forefathers, because His name was to be proclaimed shortly after His birth at the time of circumcision. [For a discussion of the power in the name of Yehovah and Yeshua, see Appendix #4, "Yehovah and Yeshua."]

**Luke 2:21—And when eight days were completed for the circumcision of the child, His name was called Yeshua, the name given by the angel before He was conceived in the womb.**

His name is Yeshua. He was called by this name when He was circumcised. Yeshua is the God-Man-Angel who was born into this world as Messiah to save us of our sins. He is the one who appeared to our forefathers and made covenant with them by circumcision (**Gen. 17:1-14**). When He was conceived, His divine personage was joined to the seed of Miriam. He existed before as the divine angel, but the divine-human union in Yeshua was a new reality that came into being only at His birth. The Angel of Yehovah who demanded circumcision of Abraham was later to be circumcised Himself when He was born into the earth as a man.

Why is this important to us today? Why was this God-Man-Angel not given a name until He was born into the world of men? Why was Yeshua's name proclaimed specifically at the time of circumcision? The answers to these questions are quite challenging, both to Jews and to Christians.

Let's look at the challenge to the Jewish worldview first. God appeared to our forefathers in the form of a God-Man-Angel. The God of Abraham, Isaac and Jacob is not a detached and distant deity, whom we cannot know or feel. He is closer than Mount Sinai; He does more than make laws and set rules; He is not a pillar of fire and cloud. He is personal, intimate, and involved in our lives. He appeared to our forefathers in the form of a Man and an Angel, and made covenant with them (**Gen. 15:18; 17:2; Exod. 2:24**).

The second part of the challenge to the Jewish worldview is that this El Shaddai, God-Man-Angel, is none other than Yeshua. Yes, the one that we have been rejecting for 2,000 years. His figure has towered over our people throughout our history, whether we have liked it or not. It is not a coincidence that our 2,000 year exile started immediately after our rejection of His message. Believing in Yeshua is the correct and logical continuation of faith in the same God that Abraham, Isaac and Jacob believed in.

The third part of the challenge to the Jewish world has to do with how we view the covenants made by our forefathers. Through those covenants, we became the chosen people. Through those covenants, we were given the land of Israel. Through those covenants, we receive heavenly and earthly blessings.

Yet who made those covenants with Abraham, Isaac and Jacob? It was this God-Man-Angel we have been studying about in these chapters. The original covenants that define our people were made with God in His Man-Angel form. That figure was Yeshua before He was born into this earth. He is the one who made covenant with our forefathers.

We are the chosen people. Our chosen-ness was defined by the covenants of the patriarchs. Those covenants were made with Yeshua. Our chosen-ness has no meaning without a relationship of faith with the God-Man-Angel who cut the covenant with our forefathers. Our chosen-ness as a people is determined through our relationship with Yeshua. Without Yeshua, our very identity as Jews, as Israelis, as the chosen people, loses its purpose.

Let us compare this point to the example of marriage. My wife took on my family name when we were married. She used to be Betty Kirshbaum. Now she is Betty Intrater. Her new name, identity and role as a wife and mother would lose its meaning without our relationship. If she divorced me, there would be no purpose in continuing to call herself Betty Intrater. The same is true for me. My role as a father and a husband would have no meaning outside of my marital covenant with Betty.

In a similar way, it is impossible for Israel to fulfill its covenant purpose without Yeshua. Our chosen-ness is not based on racial superiority. We are chosen because we have a covenant with El Shaddai. Jewish identity without that "covenant-cutting God-Man" has no purpose. Without Yeshua, we are proclaiming to be "sons of the covenant" without the partner who cut the covenant in the first place.

The fourth part of the challenge to the Jewish worldview is the connection between the land of Israel and the person of Yeshua. (We will deal with that issue more in Section Three.) Ownership of the land of Israel was given by covenant to Abraham, Isaac and Jacob. Those land covenants were made with the God-Man-Angel, whom our forefathers believed in. That figure was Yeshua. The covenantal right of the Jewish people to the land of Israel originates in a covenant with Yeshua.

The return of the Jewish people to the land of Israel since the end of the nineteenth century is not just a matter of history or politics. It is an issue of covenant and prophecy. Modern "political correctness" sees no divine mandate for our people to live in our ancient homeland. That mandate comes from the Bible. Our "right" to be in this land is based on our ancient covenants, and those covenants were made with Yeshua.

As we Jewish people turn in faith to our own Messiah, our identity as the chosen people comes into fullness (**Rom. 11:15**). Through Yeshua our restoration to the land of Israel will come into its full purpose as well (**Luke 13:34-35; 19:41-44; 21:23-24**).

Our identity and our land were given to us by covenant. The maker of that covenant was the God-Man-Angel whose name since His birth is Yeshua. Circumcision is the sign of that covenant. The circumcision is connected to the covenant, and the covenant is connected to Yeshua. Yeshua entered into the "Abrahamic" covenant through circumcision just the way Abraham did. That's why Yeshua's name was announced at the time of His circumcision.

When a father arranges for his son to be circumcised, he recites the blessing that he has caused his son to enter the Abrahamic covenant. When Yeshua was circumcised, He became committed to the covenant with Abraham. He had already been committed to the covenant with Abraham on the divine side (when He walked through the cut pieces in **Gen. 15:17**). At circumcision He became committed to the Abrahamic covenant on the human side.

Yeshua's circumcision demonstrates His commitment to the covenants with the Jewish people. The fact that His name was proclaimed at the time of circumcision demonstrates that Yeshua's identity as a human being is connected to a covenant commitment to the Jewish people.

The idea that Yeshua is the God-Man-Angel who made covenant with Abraham, Isaac and Jacob is therefore equally challenging to the Christian worldview. This challenge affects a Christian's attitude towards the Jewish people, towards the land of Israel, and towards the covenants cut with our forefathers.

A true born-again Christian has a covenant with God through Yeshua. That covenant provided forgiveness of sins and eternal life. Yet over 1,000 years before the cross, that same Yeshua cut covenant with Abraham, Isaac and Jacob. He is the one who made the Jews to be the chosen people. He is the one who declared Israel to be the promised Holy Land.

A Christian has salvation by faith in Yeshua through the New Covenant. However, Yeshua has a previous covenant with the Jewish people. Yeshua promised to give eternal life to all who believe. Although, long before that He also promised to give the land of Israel to the Jewish people. What does that mean to the Christian world today?

Let's use the example of a business contract. A person offers to make a contract to buy your business. However, you have a previous partner in the company. When it comes time to sign the contract, you must take into account the commitments you already made to your previous partner. If the new contract violates the previous contract, then the new contract is invalid.

When a company buys out another company, the new company has to recognize the contracts that the old company had with its previous employees and customers. In a similar way, for the New Covenant to maintain its integrity, it must remain faithful to the previous commitments given in the Old Covenant. The New Covenant promises to the Church require God's faithfulness to the Old Covenant promises made to the people of Israel.

The same principle also applies to governments. A new government may take control in a country; however, the new government must recognize treaty obligations made by the previous government in the name of the country. The covenants of a "new" government must recognize the "old" covenants of the previous government.

All true Christians come into a covenant relationship with Yeshua. And Yeshua has a previous covenant with the people of Israel. A Christian might say that God's covenants to Israel no longer have validity because our people have rejected Him. That is not accurate. God's promises are conditional, and our people have broken God's covenants. But, God's word is still eternally valid. Even if we have been unfaithful to our covenants, God is still faithful to His promises. The issue is not our lack of righteousness. The issue is the covenant faithfulness of God.

### Romans 15:8-9

**Now I say that the Messiah has become a servant to the circumcised because of the faithfulness of God, in order to fulfill the promises that were given to the forefathers, and so that the Gentiles will praise God for His compassion.**

Yeshua was circumcised and lived as a Torah-observant Jew to demonstrate the faithfulness of God to our people. Yeshua is a faithful husband, even if we have been an unfaithful wife (a central theme of the book of Hosea). If He will not be faithful to Israel, how will He be faithful to the Church?

In Jeremiah 31, God promises a New Covenant to provide forgiveness of sins and to write the Torah on our hearts. In that same chapter He also promises to preserve the Jewish people. The New Covenant promises are found in verses 31 to 34. The promises of preservation to the nation of Israel are found in verses 35 to 37.

**Jeremiah 31:35-37**

**Thus says Yehovah, Who gives the sun for a light by day, the ordinances of the moon and the stars for a light by night…**

**"If those ordinances depart from before Me," says Yehovah, "then the seed of Israel shall also cease from being a nation before Me forever."**

**Thus says Yehovah: "If the heavens above can be measured, and the foundations of the earth below searched out, I will also cast off all the seed of Israel for all that they have done."**

כֹּה אָמַר יְהוָה נֹתֵן שֶׁמֶשׁ לְאוֹר יוֹמָם חֻקֹּת יָרֵחַ
וְכוֹכָבִים לְאוֹר לָיְלָה...

אִם־יָמֻשׁוּ הַחֻקִּים הָאֵלֶּה מִלְּפָנַי נְאֻם־יְהוָה גַּם זֶרַע
יִשְׂרָאֵל יִשְׁבְּתוּ מִהְיוֹת גּוֹי לְפָנַי כָּל־הַיָּמִים: אִם־יִמַּדּוּ
שָׁמַיִם מִלְמַעְלָה וְיֵחָקְרוּ מוֹסְדֵי־אֶרֶץ לְמָטָּה גַּם־אֲנִי
אֶמְאַס בְּכָל־זֶרַע יִשְׂרָאֵל עַל־כָּל־אֲשֶׁר עָשׂוּ

There is a triangular covenant here. The New Covenant connects the forgiveness of sins to the preservation of the nation of Israel, which is in turn connected to the preservation of natural creation. The creation of the world was made by covenant; the chosenness of the nation of Israel was made by covenant; and eternal salvation to all believers was made by covenant. These three are linked together by covenant.

Covenant demands that either all three be true, or none of them. This is a secret spiritual root as to why both the Nazis and the Islamic Jihad set a goal to exterminate the Jewish people. If they had succeeded in destroying our people, then the New Covenant and the created order would have been in jeopardy.

One day my friend Lou Engle asked me to explain the importance of Israel in the plan of God. I asked him, "Do you see issues like abortion and homosexuality as covenantal issues?" He said, "Certainly." I said, "Well, the issues concerning Israel are covenantal as well." The issue is not so much Israel per se, as it is the faithfulness of God toward Israel. The issue is God's faithfulness to His covenants, not racial superiority.

A Christian's salvation is dependent on God's covenantal faithfulness. God has a previous covenant with the people of Israel. As Israel's destiny and identity lack validity without faith in Yeshua; so does a Christian's faith in Yeshua lack validity without recognizing God's covenant faithfulness to the Jewish people.

I am not saying that someone is not saved without being committed to the Jewish people. I am saying that Christians' salvation is based on covenant with the same El Shaddai God who made covenant with Abraham, Isaac and Jacob many years earlier. If God is faithful to one, then He will be faithful to the other.

It is equally shocking for a Christian to hear that salvation is based on a covenant which presumes a commitment to Israel, as it is for a Jew to hear that the preservation of our nation is based on a covenant which was cut with our people by Yeshua. The covenant is valid in both directions.

Did you know that one day Yeshua (as Yehovah in His human form) tried to kill Moses? While that may sound preposterous, here is the passage:

**Exodus 4:24-26**

**And it came to pass on the way, at the inn that Yehovah met him and sought to kill him. Then Zipporah took a sharp stone and cut off the foreskin of her son and touched it to Moses' feet, and said, "You are a blood husband to me now!" So He let him go.**

וַיְהִי בַדֶּרֶךְ בַּמָּלוֹן וַיִּפְגְּשֵׁהוּ יְהוָה וַיְבַקֵּשׁ הֲמִיתוֹ:
וַתִּקַּח צִפֹּרָה צֹר וַתִּכְרֹת אֶת־עָרְלַת בְּנָהּ וַתַּגַּע לְרַגְלָיו
וַתֹּאמֶר כִּי חֲתַן־דָּמִים אַתָּה לִי:
וַיִּרֶף מִמֶּנּוּ

Moses was the great deliverer of the people of Israel. He had personal prophecies, spiritual authority, and an ordained mission from God. There was just one problem; Moses forgot that his great spiritual mission was due to God's faithfulness to His covenants with Abraham, Isaac and Jacob (**Exod. 2:24**). Circumcising his son was the sign of that covenant. Without that covenant, Moses was a "dead man." Great spirituality does not eliminate the need for covenant faithfulness. Yeshua was circumcised to show God's faithfulness to His covenants.

[Does this mean that a Christian needs to be circumcised? No (Gal. 6:15). However, a Christian should be circumcised in his heart (Rom. 2:29).]

Yeshua was given His name at circumcision. He was circumcised to fulfill God's covenant faithfulness to the people of Israel. Yeshua had to be faithful to the covenant with Abraham, because He was the one who offered that covenant in the first place. Yeshua was circumcised as a covenant son of Abraham. Yeshua became part of the Abrahamic covenant. He cut covenant with the Jewish people through circumcision. Yeshua was and still is faithful to that covenant.

Yeshua made the covenants with Abraham, Isaac and Jacob. The same Yeshua made the New Covenant of salvation to all who will believe. The promises of the Abrahamic covenant are part of the foundation of the New Covenant. The promises of the New Covenant to the Christian are integrally connected with Yeshua's faithfulness to the Jewish people in the Old Covenant.

In conclusion, Yeshua was circumcised to show God's faithfulness to His own covenants. Both Jews and Christians can rejoice in that fact. Covenant faithfulness is an essential attribute of biblical faith. Since Yeshua made the original covenant with Abraham, the Jewish people will find the full meaning of their own identity and destiny when they find faith in Yeshua. Since Yeshua was faithful to the Abrahamic covenant, so ought Christians demonstrate a covenant faithfulness to the Jewish people as well.

# PART TWO

## The Exodus

---

In this section, we examine the appearances of God to Moses and the people of Israel at the time of the Exodus.

In this period the appearances of the Divine Messenger occur primarily in the form of an angel—The Angel of Yehovah. We will explore the connection between that Angel and the Messiah of the New Covenant.

We also consider how those appearances affect our understanding of the Ten Commandments and the Moral Law in general.

# CHAPTER FOUR
## The Angel of Yehovah

We come now to the period of the Exodus from Egypt. Moses had numerous encounters with the God-Man-Angel who appeared to the patriarchs. Moses first saw Him in the burning bush.

Moses had grown up as a prince in Egypt, somewhat concealing his ethnic identity and background. At age forty, he fled to Midian after a failed attempt to be the savior of his people. At age eighty, he had the encounter at the burning bush where God called him to go back to Egypt to set His people free.

**Exodus 3:2—And the Angel of Yehovah appeared to him in a flame of fire from the midst of the bush.**

וַיֵּרָא מַלְאַךְ יְהוָֹה אֵלָיו בְּלַבַּת־אֵשׁ מִתּוֹךְ הַסְּנֶה

Moses does not have an encounter with a burning bush, but with the Angel of Yehovah who appeared to him inside the flame of the bush. The Hebrew reader would notice that the expression for "appeared unto him" is exactly the same as all the appearances to Abraham.

The appearance of this Angel in a form of fire or glory is a new revelation at this point of covenant history. It had not happened previously to any of the patriarchs in the land of Canaan.

In verse two, the divine messenger is referred to as the Angel of Yehovah. However, immediately afterwards, this same messenger is called simply Yehovah or God (Elohim).

**Exodus 3:4—So when Yehovah saw that he turned aside to look, God called to him from the midst of the bush and said, "Moses, Moses!" And he said, "Here I am."**

וַיַּרְא יְהוָֹה כִּי סָר לִרְאוֹת וַיִּקְרָא אֵלָיו אֱלֹהִים מִתּוֹךְ
הַסְּנֶה וַיֹּאמֶר מֹשֶׁה מֹשֶׁה וַיֹּאמֶר הִנֵּנִי:

Notice the parallel expression of "from the midst of the bush." How can we understand this? Were there two figures in the midst of the bush? Not likely. Did the Angel and God switch places between verse 2 and 4? Not likely. Was the Angel just standing there without speaking; and then the voice of God came separately through the bush? Not likely.

It is clearly the Angel who is speaking. A reasonable response might be that the Angel spoke ON BEHALF of God. That is closer to the truth, but it is not exactly what the text says. It says that Elohim spoke from the midst of the bush; God spoke. The only unbiased way to interpret this passage is that the same figure who spoke with Moses is called the Angel of Yehovah in verse 2 and Elohim (God) in verse 4. [The rabbis struggled with this paradox in the Passover Seder in the section called "I Myself and not an angel."]

This still leaves us with two possibilities. The first is that the Angel of Yehovah is not divine but is allowed to be called God because of his mission. The second is that this figure is a special personality; He is at the same time a messenger from God and yet divine Himself— divine enough to be called both Elohim and Yehovah.

The first possibility is partially correct and covers enough of the evidence to be somewhat acceptable. However, it does not account for the total interchangeability between the names Angel, Elohim and Yehovah. Nor does it cover the fullness of the authority in which this messenger speaks and commands in the first person form.

Let us remember that this appearance at the burning bush includes enormous statements of divinity, such as **"I am that I am" (v. 14)** and **"Say, Yehovah the God of your forefathers appeared unto me" (v. 16)**. In other words, this Angel doesn't just speak on behalf of God as a messenger. He acts, reacts and interacts as God Himself.

We were challenged by the figure that appeared to Abraham in Genesis 18. The divine figure was so corporeally human in form yet totally God-Elohim-Yehovah in all that He said and did. Here as well we have the seemingly impossible combination of a figure who is clearly an Angel-Messenger from God, and yet at the same time totally God-Elohim-Yehovah. In Genesis 18 the combination was of God and man. Here in Exodus 3 the combination is of God and angel.

Let us take another example of the appearance of this Angel, alias Yehovah, to Moses. This time we look at the crossing of the Red Sea. Here, instead of a burning bush, we have a pillar of fire and smoke. Again, the Angel-Yehovah is appearing in a form of glory and fire that was not revealed to the patriarchs in Canaan.

**Exodus 13:21—And Yehovah went before them by day in a pillar of cloud...**

וַיהֹוָה הֹלֵךְ לִפְנֵיהֶם יוֹמָם בְּעַמּוּד עָנָן

**Exodus 14:19—And the Angel of God, who went before the camp of Israel, moved and went behind them; and the pillar of cloud went from before them and stood behind them.**

וַיִּסַּע מַלְאַךְ הָאֱלֹהִים הַהֹלֵךְ לִפְנֵי מַחֲנֵה יִשְׂרָאֵל וַיֵּלֶךְ מֵאַחֲרֵיהֶם וַיִּסַּע עַמּוּד הֶעָנָן מִפְּנֵיהֶם וַיַּעֲמֹד מֵאַחֲרֵיהֶם:

**Exodus 14:24—Yehovah looked out at the camp of Egypt from the pillar of fire and cloud.**

וַיַּשְׁקֵף יְהֹוָה אֶל־מַחֲנֵה מִצְרַיִם בְּעַמּוּד אֵשׁ וְעָנָן

These three verses in the same passage describe a figure who is maneuvering about in order to protect and guide Israel. The figure is traveling around from within the pillar of fire and cloud.

In verse 13:21, He is called Yehovah.

In verse 14:19, He is called the Angel of God.

In verse 14:24, He is called Yehovah.

One could try to interpret this in many ways to juggle between the cloud, the fire, the Angel, Yehovah, God, the Angel of God—all in an attempt to avoid the obvious contextual meaning of the passage: There is a special figure that led the children of Israel out of Egypt. He did so within a pillar of fire and cloud. He was at the same time both an Angel and God.

The reason why the Genesis passages call Him a "man" and the Exodus passages call Him an "angel" is that in Genesis He was seen openly in a human-like form. In the Exodus passages He is not seen openly, but concealed by the cloud. To the patriarchs He appeared in a form without fire and glory; whereas in the Exodus passages He appeared in a form with fire and glory.

There is a general pattern in Scriptures, that within the land of Israel, this figure usually appears as a man in a non-glorified form; whereas in the nations outside of Israel, He appears as an angel in a glorified form. We will touch upon that difference later in section five.

The point is that He can't be called a man in the Exodus passages because they don't see Him in a human-like form. They cannot see Him—not because He is un-seeable, but because He is filled with power to do the miraculous work at hand. That degree of power would have harmed the people if they looked at Him straight on.

[**Note on Original Hebraic Text:** Most of the Bible translations are excellent. The insights that one receives from the original language are usually small details that help to give some perspective but do not change the overall understanding of the text. In Israel we use the original Hebrew text of the Tanakh, and a reconstructed Hebrew version of the New Covenant. We do this because our teachings are designed for native Israelis.

The biblical text is not always easy to work with. The translators have provided a huge service by making the text readable. Even for someone whose knowledge of biblical Hebrew is strong, translations need to be considered occasionally in order to deal with certain words or phrases. (My favorite English version is the New King James with center cross references.)

At this time, we want to introduce and analyze one point of Hebrew language that does happen to be quite significant. Please bear with us as it is a little technical.]

There is a grammatical form in both biblical and modern Hebrew called "s'michut" — סמיכות. The word "s'michut" means to put two things closely together, so that they touch one another. This grammatical form is made up of two words put together. S'michut joins two nouns so that they define one another mutually and become one unit together.

To take an example from English, you might find something similar in such paired nouns as: ball game, door knob, piano stool, etc. In English the first noun turns into an adjective describing the second noun. Ball game is a game not a ball; the ball describes what kind of game it is. Let's call this form "paired nouns."

The paired nouns in Hebrew are similar but slightly different. The first difference is that the order is reversed: the second noun describes the first. The meanings of the two nouns merge together. They become virtually one word, or similar to a hyphenated word, like the word ball-game, door-knob, piano-stool.

The merging of the two is also emphasized because the vowels of the first word become shortened, so that the two words are spoken together in a single rhythmic pattern. A parallel might be b'll-game, d'r-knob, p'no-stool.

The paired nouns may be used either in a generic sense or to identify a proper noun. It might be any ball game, but it also might refer to a specific game, like "super-bowl" or "world-cup." Making the paired nouns into a specific name instead of a common noun is done by inserting the syllable "ha" (meaning "the") before the second noun, or by making the second noun a proper name. A parallel might be ball-the-game or "game-Wimbeldon."

Why is this technical detail so important? Because in the expression "the angel of the Lord," the "s'michut" form is always used. The Hebrew does not say "the angel of the Lord" but "angel-

Yehovah" — מלאך יהוה. The two words are joined together. The words "of" and "the" are NOT found in the original. In addition, in the angel-Yehovah paired noun, the second noun, Yehovah, is a proper name.

From this construct we come to two conclusions:

1.   Angel and Yehovah are joined into one unit.

2.   Angel Yehovah is a proper name, not a generic noun.

[A similar analysis of the s'michut form of the name "angel-Yehovah" was published as early as 1881 by Alexander McCaul in his book, *Angel of the Covenant* (reprinted by Keren Ahavah, Jerusalem, 2004).] Taking these two points a step further:

1.   It is impossible to separate the meaning of Angel from the meaning of Yehovah and vice versa. They are one and the same. The Angel is Yehovah, and Yehovah is the Angel.

2.   This is not a category which can apply to any of the other angels who come from Yehovah, but rather the proper name of a specific Angel called Yehovah.

The word Angel merges together with the proper name Yehovah. It might be better translated as Angel-YHVH, Yahweh-Angel, or Yehovah Angel. All those options would be acceptable. For our study in this book, from this point forward, we will use the name "Angel-Yehovah." (Again, for a discussion of Yahweh versus Yehovah, see Appendix #3.)

In order to simplify the point: The paired-noun grammatical form makes the expression "Angel of the Lord" to be 1) proper, and 2) merged.

1)   **Proper**—While it could be argued that Angel-Yehovah is any one of a number of angels sent from God, the grammatical form points to it being a proper noun. It is THE Angel-Yehovah, not ANY angel from Yehovah. I do not know of even one example in the entire Hebrew Bible in which the term Angel-Yehovah is in "s'michut" form,

where the context demands that it is referring to a generic angel, or one of a group of angels.

2) **Merged**—The two nouns, Angel and Yehovah, modify one another. This is not a "ball" and a "game" but a "ball-game." It is a "ball"—type of game. This is not just an angel, but a Yehovah-type angel. The two terms cannot be separated from one another. The nature of this angel is determined by the name Yehovah. Angel and Yehovah are paired noun partners.

This grammatical structure fits perfectly the description of the figure that appeared to our prophets and patriarchs. The "s'michut" is so unusual and so fitting and so perfect, that I cannot escape the impression that this grammatical form was sovereignly predestined and planned by God for the primary purpose of describing this one Person in the Hebrew Bible.

It is a unique grammatical form to define a unique individual. There is no one else like Him. A special grammatical construct was needed to be able to name Him. No man fits that category; no angel fits that category; even God our Heavenly Father does not fit that category.

The plan of salvation and the destiny of the human race demand that the Messiah be a combination of God and man. The "s'michut" has a dual form because the Angel-Yehovah has a dual nature. The dual form matches perfectly His dual nature.

The s'michut form is a Hebrew grammatical structure. Therefore, what we are saying about Angel-Yehovah does not apply to the New Testament texts, which were written in Greek. Since Angel-Yehovah is a particular Hebraic term, it cannot appear in the Greek text.

Furthermore, there was only one Angel-Yehovah, who was Yeshua. Once He is born on earth, no one else can ever fulfill that role. The category of Angel-Yehovah does not fit any appearance in the New Covenant. Theologically, that category doesn't exist anymore. All angels in the New Covenant are angels from God; they are not divine; they are on assigned missions.

The Angel-Yehovah has been born into a human body forever. He can never go back to that pre-birth condition. He who was the unnamed and mysterious Angel-Yehovah of ancient Israel has now become Yeshua the Messiah, Son of God and Son of David (**Rom. 1:3-4**), for all to know openly by faith.

# CHAPTER FIVE
## *Who Wrote the Ten Commandments?*

It was Angel-Yehovah who appeared to Moses at the burning bush. It was Angel-Yehovah who split the Red Sea and brought the children of Israel out from Egypt. It was also Angel-Yehovah who met with Moses on Mount Sinai.

We started with the question of whether a human can see God. There are many biblical warnings against seeing God in His glorified form. However, here is another biblical example where human beings did see the God of Israel. In this case there were seventy-four (74!) leaders of Israel who went up on Mount Sinai and saw God.

**Exodus 24:9-11—Then Moses, Aharon, Nadav, Avihu, and seventy of the elders of Israel went up and they saw the God of Israel. And beneath His feet was like a work of sapphire pavement, and it was like the very heavens in its clarity. But on the nobles of the children of Israel He did not lay His hand. So they saw God, and they ate and drank.**

וַיַּעַל מֹשֶׁה וְאַהֲרֹן נָדָב וַאֲבִיהוּא וְשִׁבְעִים מִזִּקְנֵי
יִשְׂרָאֵל: וַיִּרְאוּ אֵת אֱלֹהֵי יִשְׂרָאֵל וְתַחַת רַגְלָיו כְּמַעֲשֵׂה
לִבְנַת הַסַּפִּיר וּכְעֶצֶם הַשָּׁמַיִם לָטֹהַר: אֶל־אֲצִילֵי בְּנֵי
יִשְׂרָאֵל לֹא שָׁלַח יָדוֹ וַיֶּחֱזוּ אֶת־הָאֱלֹהִים וַיֹּאכְלוּ
וַיִּשְׁתּוּ:

This is an unprecedented event. The elders see God in a bodily human form but also in glorified power. Such closeness to divine power was dangerous. It is clear that they were aware of the danger, because they took special note of the fact that God did not "lay His hand upon them."

The Angel-Yehovah in this passage again appeared in a human form. His feet and legs are mentioned (legs and feet are the same in Hebrew). Twice the passage states unequivocally that they saw God. The fact that His legs are mentioned and not His face, indicates that they did not see His face. It is likely from the context that the pillar of cloud which normally hid all of His form was in this case hiding just His upper body or His facial area.

When Angel-Yehovah is not in glorified form, His face can be seen. When He does appear with the glory power "turned on," it is His face that is the most dangerous. The glory power radiates from His face and eyes. It is God's glorified face that no man can see (**Exod. 33:20**). From God's face comes the enlightenment and radiation of the priestly blessing (**Num. 6:25**). After spending forty days in His presence, Moses' face also began to shine (**Exod. 34:29**).

A similar point is made in the New Covenant that Yeshua's face will shine like the sun (**Rev. 1:16**) and His eyes will be like a flame of fire (**Rev. 1:14; 2:18; 19:12**) [More on that in Section Five].

On Mount Sinai, Angel-Yehovah instructed the seventy-four leaders to eat and drink; I imagine they were not much in the mood for eating at the time. He asked them to eat and drink for two reasons. One, as in the case of Abraham, God was offering them a covenant meal of friendship. In the midst of all the fire-works display on Mount Sinai, Angel-Yehovah wanted them to know that His ultimate goal was not to scare them, but to bring them into intimate fellowship with Himself. He was making covenant, not just commandments; He wanted loyalty, not just laws.

The second reason was to assure them that this experience was real. As with Jacob at Peniel, God did not want them to think this was a non-material vision, or a group hallucination. He was there. He was really there. They saw Him, they were in His presence physically, and they escaped unharmed.

This passage in Exodus 24 is similar to that of the visit to Abraham in Genesis 18. It establishes the fact that the God of Israel has a form which is similar to a human being. The God of Exodus 24 is the same God as that of Genesis 18.

The God of Israel, who appeared to Abraham in a friendly, non-glorified form, appeared to Moses in terrifying, mountain-shaking form. It is one and the same Person, whether in intimate human like fellowship or in glorifying displays of majesty. That Person is the God of Israel. He is the God that our patriarchs and prophets knew and believed in. They understood that God could appear in a human form. He could come with fire power or without. He was the one on Mount Sinai. He was the one who made covenant with our forefathers, and who brought our people out of Egypt. If He was there on Mount Sinai, then He must have also been the one who wrote the Ten Commandments— **"by the finger of God"** (**Exod. 31:18**; **Deut. 9:10**).

Moses knew of the appearances of the God-Man to Abraham, Isaac and Jacob. After all, he was the one who wrote their experiences down in the book of Genesis. He must have suspected that the One who had been leading them out of Egypt was the same One who appeared to the patriarchs. However, until this moment in chapter 24, he had not seen Him.

Moses spent forty days and nights on Mount Sinai. The Angel-Yehovah wrote the Ten Commandments and explained to him all the other laws. Yet Moses had still not attained the intimacy and glory with his Creator, that he so desired. Moses descends from Mount Sinai with the Torah to find that the people have gone wild with carnality and idolatry. He is fed up and frustrated. He smashes the two tablets of the Ten Commandments that Angel-Yehovah had just written (**Exod. 32:19**)!

A civil war almost breaks out within the Israelites. The Levites kill 3,000 of the sinners (**Exod. 32:28**). After establishing order, Moses returns to the mountain for a second (!) forty-day fast. His attitude at this point is: "Look God, I've had it with leadership; I've had it with laws. Even seeing all your miracles is not enough. I want You. I want to see Your face. I want to know You. I want Your intimacy and Your glory. If You don't give me both, then find someone else."

Moses spent more time with Angel-Yehovah than any other human being. They talked for hours. Not only did He give him all the laws, He also explained to him some of the details about the history of creation, which Moses later wrote in the book of Genesis. But in all those conversations until now, Angel-Yehovah is covered with cloud. The Bible says that Moses talked with God face to face, but that did not mean that he saw Him directly in the face. This is obvious because Moses still asks to see His face.

In the other encounters until then, such as at the burning bush and at the Red Sea, the Angel-Yehovah had been covered either with fire or cloud. Now Moses wanted more. He wanted to see His face and His fire.

**Exodus 33:11—So Yehovah spoke to Moses face to face, as a man speaks to his friend...**

וְדִבֶּר יְהֹוָה אֶל־מֹשֶׁה פָּנִים אֶל־פָּנִים כַּאֲשֶׁר יְדַבֵּר אִישׁ אֶל־רֵעֵהוּ

[Many make the mistake here to think that the phrase "face to face" means that Moses already saw His face. What is being described here is their verbal communication. They "spoke" face to face. It is not referring to direct visible sight. This can be proved by comparing the phrase "spoke face to face" in **Deuteronomy 5:4** referring to all the people at Mount Sinai, none of whom saw His face directly. There the expression also means that they heard His voice directly, but did not see His face. At this point, Moses had spoken directly and openly with God in the cloud, but had still not seen His face.]

It is possible for a man to look God in the face if the glory is turned down. Or, a man can see God in His glory power on the condition that the cloud would cover God's face. Moses is not satisfied with either of those two partial options, and says he wants to see God's face directly with the glory power as well. "Remove the cloud. Turn up the power. Let me see Your face." Moses was quite bold.

**Exodus 33:13—Now therefore, I pray, if I have found favor in Your eyes, show me now your way, that I may know You...**

אִם־נָא מָצָאתִי חֵן בְּעֵינֶיךָ הוֹדִעֵנִי נָא אֶת־דְּרָכֶךָ וְאֵדָעֲךָ

In spiritual language, Moses was asking to see God's glorified face. This is apparent because in the next verse Angel-Yehovah responds:

**Exodus 33:14—And He said, "My face will go before you, and I will give you rest."**

וַיֹּאמַר:  פָּנַי יֵלֵכוּ, וַהֲנִחֹתִי לָךְ.

Moses refuses to accept this non-committal response. So he presses in.

**Exodus 33:15, 18—If Your face does not go *with us*, do not bring us up from here… show me Your glory.**

אִם־אֵין פָּנֶיךָ הֹלְכִים אַל־תַּעֲלֵנוּ מִזֶּה: …הַרְאֵנִי נָא אֶת־כְּבֹדֶךָ:

[Unfortunately, most versions translate the word "face" here incorrectly as "presence" and miss what Moses was saying. The original clearly states "face." Moses wanted to see God's face in glorified form.]

Then Angel-Yehovah makes the point clear. You may speak with Me as a friend and see My face when the glory is down. Or you can talk with Me at a close distance (face to face, as it were), when My glory is up. However, in that case My face will have to be covered by the cloud. Why? Because no one can see My face in all its glory and be able to withstand that much power. It would kill him.

**Exodus 33:20—You cannot see My face; for no man shall see Me and live.**

לֹא תוּכַל לִרְאֹת אֶת־פָּנָי כִּי לֹא־יִרְאַנִי הָאָדָם וָחָי:

So Angel-Yehovah offers a solution to Moses. To look at His face directly in full power is just not possible. So He put him in a crevice in a big rock and turned sideways so that Moses could at least see His form from behind.

**Exodus 33:21-23—And Yehovah said, "Here is a place by Me, and you shall stand there on the rock. So it will be, while My**

**glory passes by, that I will put you in the cleft of the rock, and I will cover you with My hand until I pass by. Then I will remove My hand and you will see My backsides; but My face will not be seen.**

הִנֵּה מָקוֹם אִתִּי וְנִצַּבְתָּ עַל־הַצּוּר: וְהָיָה בַּעֲבֹר כְּבֹדִי
וְשַׂמְתִּיךָ בְּנִקְרַת הַצּוּר וְשַׂכֹּתִי כַפִּי עָלֶיךָ עַד־עָבְרִי:
וַהֲסִרֹתִי אֶת־כַּפִּי וְרָאִיתָ אֶת־אֲחֹרָי וּפָנַי לֹא יֵרָאוּ:

All the prophets and patriarchs, no matter how spiritual, were left with one of two options to see Angel-Yehovah. One choice was in a human form with the power turned down, as in the case with Abraham at the oaks of Mamre. The other option was as the glorified Angel. In that case, He had to be covered with a cloud, or be at a great distance.

The greater option still exists of seeing Him directly and in full power. That option was only reached by two men. The first was Stephan, the first martyr (**Acts 6-7**). At the moment of his death, he saw the heavens opened with Yeshua standing at the right hand of glory (**Acts 7:55**). In this case Stephan was about to leave his physical body anyway, so it didn't do much damage for him to see Yeshua in full glory.

The second person to reach that revelation was John on the Isle of Patmos. In the last book of the Bible, the full revelation finally comes. John got what both Abraham and Moses longed to see. He saw Yeshua in full glory, face to face. John was already born again. He was filled with the Holy Spirit. He was Yeshua's best friend on the earth. But even then, he almost dropped dead from the experience.

He sees Yeshua with His face shining like the sun, His eyes like flames of fire, His voice like many rivers flowing, etc. (**Rev. 1:12-16**). John saw Angel-Yehovah's glorified face and almost died on the spot. Here is what John said happened at that moment:

**Revelation 1:17—And when I saw Him, I fell at His feet as dead. But He laid His right hand on me, saying, "Do not be afraid; I am the First and the Last."**

We will deal with this revelation more thoroughly in the fifth section. Here we are simply making the connection between Moses' request and John's revelation. John saw in Revelation chapter 1 what Moses was asking for in Exodus chapter 33. Moses saw the same glorified God-Man that John did; only Moses had to see Him from behind. The time was not yet fulfilled for Yeshua to be revealed in all His glory.

Neither did the rest of Yeshua's disciples reach that level of glory revelation. On the Mount of Transfiguration, Yeshua tried to show them, but they fell asleep. They were not ready to handle that much glory. God had to cover them over quickly with the cloud, so they would not be hurt by the power that was present. At the time, the disciples were terrified and almost died (**Matt. 17:6**).

The Mount of Transfiguration experience took place around 1,400 years after the Mount Sinai experience. By that time, Moses had already died and gone to heaven. In heaven, Moses was able to see Yeshua, the Angel-Yehovah, any time he desired. It is recorded that Moses even appeared on the Mount of Transfiguration with Yeshua and the disciples. So there is no need to worry about Moses. He eventually received all that he desired, and more.

### Matthew 16:28-17:9

**"Surely, I say to you, there are some standing here who shall not taste death until they see the Son of Man coming in His kingdom."**

**Now after six days Yeshua took Peter, James, and John his brother, led them up on a high mountain by themselves; and He was transfigured before them. His face shone like the sun, and His clothes became as white as the light. And behold, Moses and Elijah appeared to them, talking with Him. Then Peter answered and said to Yeshua, "Lord, it is good for us to be here; if You wish, let us make here three tabernacles: one for You, one for Moses, and one for Elijah."**

**While he was still speaking, behold, a bright cloud overshadowed them; and suddenly a voice came out of the cloud, saying, "This is My beloved Son, in whom I am well pleased. Hear Him!" And when the disciples heard it, they**

**fell on their faces and were greatly afraid. But Yeshua came and touched them and said, "Arise, and do not be afraid." When they had lifted up their eyes, they saw no one but Yeshua only.**

**Now as they came down from the mountain, Yeshua commanded them, saying, "Tell the vision to no one until the Son of Man is risen from the dead."**

Peter, James and John almost got to see what all the prophets and patriarchs longed for. However they were not ready. During all the rest of the gospels, Yeshua appears in a non-glorified form, somewhat similar to the visit with Abraham. He appeared in a non-glorified form on purpose. He gave up His glory to be able to approach mankind. (**"He who existed in the form of God, did not consider it robbery to be equal to God, yet emptied Himself and took on the form of a servant, and became like men, and was in a form like men." Phil. 2:6-7**)

Yeshua could have come to earth as He already did on Mount Sinai, full of glory and power. But then everyone would have run away from Him, just as they did back then (**Exod. 20:18-21**). The Angel-Yehovah took off His glory power and came down to get close to mankind. He not only came close, He died as a sacrifice to offer us reconciliation and forgiveness.

Notice the parallel between Moses' request on Mount Sinai, and Yeshua's desire to reveal His glory to His disciples on the Mount of Transfiguration. Moses was there both times! The cloud and the glory were there. All the elements were in place. Yet they were not ready. God still desires to show us His glory and to transform us into that glory. However, we are still not ready.

Yeshua also appeared to Saul (Paul) before he became a believer. Saul was immediately blinded. It was not that the power burned out his eyes, just the contrary. The glory would have killed him and burned out his eyes, but Yeshua did him a great favor and created the first pair of contact lenses. These lenses were opaque. They fell off his eyes three days later when he was prayed for by Hananiah.

**Acts 9:3-5—Suddenly a light from heaven shone around him. Then he fell on the ground, and heard a voice saying to him, "Saul, Saul, why are you persecuting Me?"**

**And Saul asked, "Who are You, Lord?"**

**Then the Lord said, "I am Yeshua whom you are persecuting..."**

**Acts 9:7-8—And the men who journeyed with him stood speechless, hearing a voice, but seeing no one. Then Saul arose from the ground, and when he opened his eyes, he could not see a thing.**

**Acts 9:17-18—And Hananiah went and entered the house; and laying his hands on him he said, "Saul, my brother, the Lord Yeshua who appeared to you on the road as you came, has sent me in order that you might see again and be filled with the Holy Spirit. Immediately there fell from his eyes something like scales, and he received his sight at once;**

Yeshua darkened Saul's cornea to protect his eyes. A new lens was created when Hananiah prayed, and the old layer fell away. Yeshua appeared to Saul in a glorified light-filled form as he did to John. But Saul was not ready. Yeshua protected him so that he would not be killed. In a similar way, Yeshua placed His hand over Moses so that Moses would not be injured when he saw the glory on Mount Sinai.

Yeshua as the Angel-Yehovah came on a mission in the book of Exodus. That mission demanded Him to maintain His glory power radiating at all times. Operating in that power, Yeshua delivered the people from Egypt and gave them the Torah. However, that same power made it necessary to keep the people at a far distance (**Exod. 19:12**).

When Yeshua was born into this world, He came on a different mission. The task of the gospel demanded just the opposite. He came without power in order to bring people close to Him. When He comes back the next time, it will be in full glory power again, much more like Mount Sinai than the shores of Galilee.

# CHAPTER SIX
# Yeshua and the Moral Law

If Angel-Yehovah wrote the Ten Commandments, and if Yeshua is that Angel-Yehovah, then it is He who wrote the Ten Commandments. This fact has wide-ranging implications for both Christianity and Judaism (**Exod. 19:18; Matt. 27:51**). Let's look at both sides.

There is a beautiful balance in the Scriptures between grace and law. The Jewish prayer book says that the love of God and the fear of God are one and the same. [See "Unify our hearts in love and in fear" – ויחד לבבנו לאהבה וליראה – (Morning Prayer, "Everlasting Love" – אהבת עולם).]

In the New Covenant, we see an example of that balance in Yeshua's dealing with the woman caught in adultery. He understands from the circumstances that the religious leaders were out to condemn her unfairly; since they had brought only the woman and not the man; and because she was obviously repentant of what she had done.

Yeshua rebukes her accusers by telling them that whichever one of them was without sin should throw the first stone. When they disperse, He turns to the woman and says:

**John 8:11—Neither do I condemn you; go and sin no more.**

In His masterful way, Yeshua summarizes the biblical balance of grace and justice in just a few words: "Don't condemn. Don't sin." If we take the gospel of forgiveness, and remove the absolute moral standards, then we end up with, "I do not condemn you, sin all you want to." If we take the moral standards without forgiveness, then we have just "You've sinned; you're condemned."

Forgiveness without moral law leads to humanism and crime. Moral law without forgiveness leads to religiosity and condemnation. Christianity that does not see Yeshua as the Law-giver is in danger of humanistic relativism and becoming an excuse for Western moral decadence. Judaism without the grace of Yeshua as the

Law-forgiver is in danger of legalist extremism and becoming a Jewish version of Islamic Sharia law.

In the story of the woman caught in adultery, Yeshua stoops down and writes with His finger on the ground. It is difficult not to make an immediate association between His writing with His finger on the ground (**John 8:8**) and the writing of the Ten Commandments with His finger on the tablets (**Exod. 31:18**). The same finger that wrote, "Thou shall not commit adultery" was writing now how to apply that law with grace and justice. [Compare as well the divine finger that wrote on the wall the judgment against Babylon (Dan. 5:5).]

It is possible that Yeshua wrote on the ground the commandment against adultery (**Exod. 20:14**). Or He may have written the verse that both the man and woman have to be equally punished (**Lev. 20:10**), which had been violated in this case. Or He wrote the verses which state that before the witness throws the first stone (**Deut. 13:10**), the case must be investigated fully in righteousness (**Deut. 13:15**).

The mention of Yeshua writing with His finger is a reference from John about Yeshua's authorship of the Ten Commandments. While Yeshua gave grace in this case to the woman caught in adultery, He was "harder" in another sense when He dealt with the subject in the Sermon on the Mount. There He said that adultery was not just a physical issue but one of lust of the eyes and adultery in one's imaginations (**Matt. 5:28**).

The entire Sermon on the Mount should be seen as Yeshua's application of the Ten Commandments. The one who wrote the Law on Mount Sinai is giving His authoritative interpretation of the Law on Mount Beatitude. The Sermon on the Mount makes much more sense if we see the one interpreting the commandments with the same authority as the one who wrote it. For instance, I can make editorial changes in the text of this book because I am the one writing it. The legislature that enacts a law has authority to make amendments to that law. Yeshua had authority because He was the author. What He wrote on Mount Sinai, He interpreted in the Sermon on the Mount.

Yeshua taught about murder as well. He compared murder to gossip and anger. He made the issues of character assassination and emotional abuse (**Matt. 5:22**) as part of the Law. He also decreed that motives of the heart are key factors in determining guilt. Motives of the heart were already introduced in connection with murder in the laws concerning the avenger of blood (**Num. 35:19-21**). What Yeshua taught was perfectly consistent with what went before. It was part of God's plan to develop the concepts of justice and grace in the people.

A parent will give rules to young children at an age when they cannot understand the reasons for them. As the child grows, the parent explains to the child the purpose and reasons behind the rules. Similarly, Yeshua gave the Law on Mount Sinai, and then explained the heart purpose behind it on the Mount of Beatitudes.

Yeshua also spoke of the Sabbath. In Judaism we have developed mountains of ritual rules (*halacha*) about what to do and not do. Yeshua believed that such a compendium of added ritual laws diminished the ability to observe the Sabbath in the way it had originally been intended. He summarized His approach to dealing with Sabbath laws in three simple statements:

1. **The Sabbath was made for mankind—Mark 2:27**

2. **The Son of Man is lord of the Sabbath—Mark 2:28**

3. **It is lawful to do good on the Sabbath—Mark 3:4**

(For a more extended discussion, see the Appendix #5 on "Keeping the Sabbath.")

His teaching on this subject was miraculous and revolutionary in its simplicity and purity. In addition, His teaching was more than just a commentary about the Sabbath. In the Jewish world there is a position called "Posek Ha Dor" — פוסק הדור; the top rabbi who passes judgment and determines what becomes law in his generation. Yeshua was speaking as "Posek Ha Dor." He was not suggesting law, He was setting the law. He was not making commentary about the law, He was decreeing it.

Some countries have a President of the legislature that makes the laws and a Supreme Court Chief Justice who determines what the law means. Yeshua was the President of the legislature on Mount Sinai; on Mount Beatitude, He was the Supreme Court Chief Justice. He both wrote the Law and determined how to apply it.

A foundational error in Christianity is divorcing the gospel message from basic moral standards found in the Torah. A foundational error in Judaism is divorcing the Torah from the gospel of grace found in Yeshua. The Torah leads to the Cross; and the Cross completes the Torah.

The Torah was not given in a vacuum. It was one part of four elements. The Torah set the standard of moral absolutes. The commandments of the Torah were given together with the sacrifices, which provided atonement and forgiveness for those who repented. In addition to the sacrifices was the presence of the Holy Spirit. All three of these—the moral commandments (**Exod. 20-23**), the atoning sacrifices (**Lev. 1-17**) and the Holy Spirit (**Num. 9:15-23; 11:24-30**) were given to Israel by the authority of Angel-Yehovah.

If one separates the commandments of the Torah from the forgiveness in the sacrifices, from the leading of the Holy Spirit, and from the authority of Angel-Yehovah, then the Torah becomes warped into something it was not intended to be. To summarize the proper context of the Torah:

1.  Angel-Yehovah

2.  Moral Commandments

3.  Atoning Sacrifices

4.  Holy Spirit Inspiration

Without the leading of the Holy Spirit, the rabbis must write volumes of additional commandments to guide the people. Without the atoning sacrifice of the cross, ritual symbols —such as head coverings, kissing the Mezuzah, washing hands and lighting candles—take on a superstitious level of spiritual importance. Without submitting to the authority of the Messiah who gave the Torah, the rabbis take on an exaggerated level of religious authority. (Rabbinic authority is very similar to Papal authority in that regard.)

In the New Covenant, the Torah is written on our hearts (**Jer. 31:31-34**). Although over-simplified, it could be stated: Rabbinic Judaism has kept the Torah on the outside; while Western Christianity has largely rejected the Torah. The correct biblical way to fulfill the righteousness of the Torah is to:

1.  Meditate on the heart-meaning of the Law

2.  Act according to the highest level of moral integrity

3.  Receive forgiveness through Yeshua's atoning sacrifice

4.  Obey the leading of the Holy Spirit

Religious Jews say that because we cannot obey the commandments as they are written in the Torah alone, we must have many rabbinic laws. I agree with them on the premise; I disagree on the conclusion. I agree that it is impossible just to keep the Torah. However, the answer is not myriads of additional laws on every kind of minutia. The answer is to place the Torah in the context of forgiveness of sins, the indwelling of the Holy Spirit and the lordship of the Messiah.

**John 1:17—For the Torah was given through Moses; and grace and truth came through Yeshua the Messiah.**

Yeshua fulfilled the Law in a way in which we all failed to do so. He alone never sinned. Through faith in Him and through the power of the Holy Spirit in our lives, the righteous requirements of the Law, the heart purpose of moral purity, are fulfilled in us.

**Romans 8:1-4**

**There is therefore now no condemnation to those who are in Messiah Yeshua, who do not walk according to the flesh, but according to the Spirit. For the law of the Spirit of life in Messiah Yeshua has made me free from the law of sin and death. For what the law could not do, in that it was weak through the flesh, God did by sending His own Son in the**

**likeness of sinful flesh, on account of sin: He condemned sin in the flesh, that the righteous requirement of the law might be fulfilled in us who do not walk according to the flesh but according to the Spirit.**

We do not deny the Law that Angel-Yehovah gave to Moses. We fulfill the inner purpose of the Law through faith in Yeshua; we fulfill its perfect moral standards through the leading of the Holy Spirit. (For more discussion, see Appendix #6 on the "Ladder of Gospel and Law.")

The absolute moral standards as set in the Ten Commandments are the foundation to understanding the meaning of salvation. A rich young nobleman came once to Yeshua and asked Him what he had to do to be saved. Yeshua answered:

**Matthew 19:17—If you want to enter into life, keep the commandments.**

For many Christians today, Yeshua's answer would be totally incomprehensible. However, from a biblical viewpoint, it was perfectly logical. But one might object, "I thought we were saved by believing in Yeshua?" I agree totally, but, there is no need to separate moral commandments from faith in Yeshua.

It was Yeshua in the form of Angel-Yehovah who wrote the Ten Commandments. To believe in Him is to obey Him (**Matt. 6:24; 7:22; Luke 6:46; Rom. 1:5**). To believe in Him starts with the obedience to basic moral standards. Simple obedience and moral integrity are one of the first steps of faith.

The young man then asked Yeshua which commandments He is referring to. Yeshua answered:

**Matthew 19:18—You shall not murder, You shall not commit adultery, You shall not steal, You shall not bear false witness, Honor your father and mother, and You shall love your neighbor as yourself.**

Yeshua wrote these commandments in the first place. He is telling the young man, "If you want to follow Me, start by obeying the most basic of moral commandments which I already gave you."

There is no contradiction between moral standards and the gospel—quite the contrary. If we do not see the connection between Yeshua and the Ten Commandments, we will continue with the embarrassing situation in which pastors and evangelists are committing adultery and stealing money; in which our children are disrespectful of authority, and in which we have lost the moral fiber to call our nations to repentance.

**1 John 3:4, 6-9—Everyone who sins transgresses the Torah. Sin is the transgression of the Torah... Everyone who abides in Him does not sin. Anyone who sins has not seen Him and has not known Him. Let no one deceive you: He who does righteousness is righteous, just as He is righteous. He who does sin is from the devil, for the devil has sinned from the beginning. For this reason the Son of God has been revealed: to destroy the works of the devil. Everyone who is born of God does not sin...**

The Torah defines what is sin and righteousness. The cross gives us forgiveness of sins. The Holy Spirit gave us the power of righteousness. Yeshua wrote the Ten Commandments; died on the cross, and gave us the Holy Spirit. It all fits together perfectly. [Again, for a further discussion, see Appendix #6 on "Ladder of Gospel and Law."]

**1 John 3:23—And this is His commandment: that we should believe on the name of His Son Yeshua the Messiah and love one another, as He gave us commandment.**

From a New Covenant point of view, the first commandment is to believe in Yeshua. How does that fit with the Ten Commandments? The introduction to the first of the Ten Commandments deals with the issue of faith in the Angel-Yehovah.

**Exodus 20:2—I am Yehovah your God, who brought you out of the land of Egypt.**

אָנֹכִי יְהֹוָה אֱלֹהֶיךָ אֲשֶׁר הוֹצֵאתִיךָ מֵאֶרֶץ מִצְרַיִם מִבֵּית עֲבָדִים:

The first of the Ten Commandments is: "I am Yehovah." The first commandment is to believe that a certain someone is Yehovah.

Who is that someone? It is the same one who brought us out of Egypt in the pillar of cloud. It is the same one who appeared to Moses. That someone said, "I am Yehovah." Who said that? Who wrote those words? The one who wrote those words was the Angel-Yehovah whose finger wrote the Ten Commandments. He is Yehovah God. The revelation that Angel-Yehovah is God is the beginning of all the commandments.

In New Covenant terms, to believe in Yeshua and to love our neighbor is the summary of all the commandments. Seeing Yeshua as Angel-Yehovah is the key to understanding the connection between moral law and faith in the Messiah.

The first of the Ten Commandments is not saying to believe that Yehovah is God. The people who came out of Egypt already believed that Yehovah was God. To believe that Yehovah is God was what Elijah demanded of the backslidden nation on Mount Carmel. They cried out, **"Yehovah is God, Yehovah is God"(1 Kings 18:39).**

The first of the Ten Commandments is not "Yehovah is God," but "I am Yehovah." There is a significant difference between those two statements. The Ten Commandments were given to people who already believed that Yehovah is God. The revelation that Yehovah is God was intended for those who worshiped Baal. There is a difference between the revelation of Mount Carmel and of Mount Sinai.

On Mount Carmel, Elijah spoke to those who thought Baal was God. He told them that their belief was false. Baal is not God. Yehovah is God. On Mount Sinai Moses spoke to those who already believed that Yehovah is God. He told them that the Angel-Yehovah who brought them out of Egypt and wrote the Ten Commandments, He is the one we call Yehovah. And He is our God.

The Divine Angel on Mount Sinai wrote to the people of Israel, "I am Yehovah. I am your God. I am the one who brought you out of Egypt." The Angel who brought them out of Egypt; who wrote the commandments; who accompanied them in the pillar of fire and cloud; is revealing His identity and divinity to the people of Israel. "I am He; I am the Yehovah God your forefathers have always believed in."

The Angel on the Mount called Himself Yehovah. That is the introduction and the first of the Ten Commandments. The Ten Commandments were written by the Angel-Yehovah. We believe that Angel-Yehovah was born into this world as Yeshua in the New Covenant. The conclusion is that Yeshua, in His pre-birth form as the Angel-Yehovah, declares that He is Yehovah-God. It is a statement of identity and authority. The New Covenant parallel of the first of the Ten Commandments is to believe in the lordship and divinity of Yeshua.

The moral law comes from Yeshua. On Mount Sinai, His finger wrote the Ten Commandments. On the Mount of Beatitudes, He explained the heart meaning of the Torah. On Mount Calvary, He died to forgive us of our transgressions of that Law. On the Mount of Olives, He will return to punish those who refuse that forgiveness and obedience.

**"Many will say to Me in that day, 'Lord, Lord...' Then I will tell them, 'I never knew you. Depart from Me, you doers of evil.'" (Matt. 7:22)**

**"Why do you call Me, 'Lord, Lord' and do not do what I tell you?'" (Luke 6:43)**

Since Yeshua wrote the Law, He had authority to forgive transgressions of that Law. Since He took the punishment we deserved by our transgressions, He as has the right to punish those who continue to transgress without repentance. Only one who would forgive by grace could be worthy to punish in judgment. The author became the redeemer. The redeemer will become the judge.

The Angel-Yehovah gave the Law on Mount Sinai. The law-giver of Mount Sinai became the law-forgiver of Mount Calvary. He will return one day to be the judge of the living and the dead.

# PART THREE

# The Conquest

In this section, we examine the appearances of God to Joshua and the Judges during the conquest of Canaan.

In this period we discover the appearance of the Divine Messenger as the Commander of the Armies of Yehovah. We will compare the role of that Commander to the picture of Yeshua at the Second Coming, particularly in the book of Revelation.

We will also consider how the role of Commander affects our understanding of the importance of the land of Israel and the redemption of the earth in the fulfillment of End Times' prophecies.

# CHAPTER SEVEN
## *The Commander-in-Chief*

God appeared in the form of a Man to Abraham, Isaac and Jacob, and made covenant with them. The Angel-Yehovah brought the children of Israel out of Egypt and gave them the Ten Commandments. This same God-Angel-Man then accompanied Israel as they conquered the land of Canaan. In that stage they came to know Him in yet another aspect of His character: The Commander-in-Chief of the angelic armies.

On the night before the battle of Jericho, Joshua had an amazing and vivid encounter with the God-Angel-Man.

**Joshua 5:13-15**

**And it came to pass, when Joshua was by Jericho, that he lifted his eyes and looked, and behold, a Man stood opposite him with His sword drawn in His hand.**

**And Joshua went to Him and said to Him, "Are You for us or for our adversaries?"**

**So He said, "No, but as the Commander of the army of Yehovah, I have now come."**

**And Joshua fell on His face to the earth and worshiped, and said to Him, "What does my Lord say to His servant?"**

**Then the Commander of Yehovah's Army said unto Joshua, "Take your sandal off your foot, for the place where you stand is holy." And Joshua did so.**

וַיְהִי בִּהְיוֹת יְהוֹשֻׁעַ בִּירִיחוֹ וַיִּשָּׂא עֵינָיו וַיַּרְא
וְהִנֵּה־אִישׁ עֹמֵד לְנֶגְדּוֹ וְחַרְבּוֹ שְׁלוּפָה בְּיָדוֹ וַיֵּלֶךְ
יְהוֹשֻׁעַ אֵלָיו וַיֹּאמֶר לוֹ הֲלָנוּ אַתָּה אִם־לְצָרֵינוּ: וַיֹּאמֶר
לֹא כִּי אֲנִי שַׂר־צְבָא־יְהוָה עַתָּה בָאתִי וַיִּפֹּל יְהוֹשֻׁעַ
אֶל־פָּנָיו אַרְצָה וַיִּשְׁתָּחוּ וַיֹּאמֶר לוֹ מָה אֲדֹנִי מְדַבֵּר
אֶל־עַבְדּוֹ: וַיֹּאמֶר שַׂר־צְבָא יְהוָה אֶל־יְהוֹשֻׁעַ שַׁל־נַעַלְךָ

מֵעַל רַגְלֶךָ כִּי הַמָּקוֹם אֲשֶׁר אַתָּה עֹמֵד עָלָיו קֹדֶשׁ הוּא
וַיַּעַשׂ יְהוֹשֻׁעַ כֵּן:

This passage takes my breath away. The words "Commander of the Army of Yehovah" have a hyphen between them in the Hebrew, and there are only three words, with no prepositions or articles. It is one word, or one name. To get the feel of it, we could translate this phrase as "**Yehovah-Army-Commander.**" In modern terms, we would call Him, "Commander-in-Chief."

In Israel, the commander over all the Israeli Defense Forces is called "Ramat-Kal," or "Head of the General Command," similar to what is called in the United States "Head of the Joint Chiefs of Staff." In the previous chapter, we saw Yeshua as the President of the Legislature and the Chief Justice of the Supreme Court. Now it is time to know Him as the Commander in Chief of the Armed Forces.

Who is this Man? He can't be God our Heavenly Father because He is referred to as a man. He can't be an ordinary angel because Joshua calls Him Lord and worships Him. This "Man" tells Joshua to take his shoes off, because the place where he is standing is holy. That phrase is quoting exactly what the Angel-Yehovah said to Moses at the burning bush (**Exod. 3:5**). He is unequivocally stating, "I am the same one that appeared to Moses in the bush."

What seems surprising is the speed and ease at which Joshua agrees to worship Him and obey Him. Apparently Joshua recognized Him from before. Joshua was with Moses much of the time that Moses spent with the Angel-Yehovah in the wilderness. At times Joshua even stayed in the tent of meeting after Moses had left (**Exod. 33:11**). Joshua didn't recognize Him at first because He came in a slightly different role, but the moment Angel-Yehovah spoke to him, he knew right away.

What a challenging and inspiring moment! This Person is:

1. **A Man:** As clearly stated in verse 13

2. **An Army Commander:** As defined in verse 14

3.  **An Angel:** As a member of the angelic armies

4.  **God:** As equivalent to the I AM of the burning bush

5.  **Lord:** As Joshua worships Him

The combination of all those qualities is a mathematical set that has no possible members in it—except one. This mixture of attributes is what the New Covenant attributes to Yeshua alone. The only logical conclusion is that this Commander whom Joshua met must be Yeshua.

The name Joshua in Hebrew is Yehoshua and is essentially the same name as Yeshua. (Yeshua is a shortened form of Yehoshua). Yeshua is named after Yehoshua, or vice versa. This is a meeting between Joshua and Jesus. I call it the meeting between big **"J"** and little **"J."** There is a parallel in their roles. Yeshua is an image of Yehoshua, and Yehoshua is an image of Yeshua.

[**Note:** In this passage is also a poignant one-word teaching on the sovereignty of God. Like Joshua, we want to know whether God is on OUR side or not. We treat him almost like a fan in the World Cup. "Are You for Spain or Holland?" But Angel-Yehovah doesn't say whether He is on Israel's side or their enemies'. He simply says, "No." The issue is not whether He is on our side, but whether we are on His side. He is not "playing sides." When we are on His side, He is on our side. He is the Sovereign Lord. When Israel sinned, God punished them. When they walked in covenant, He fought for them. In this case, He was indeed fighting on their behalf.]

If we meditate on this passage, we will immediately notice that something is missing. He is the commander of the army, but there is no army. Where is the army that He is the commander of? The prophet Elisha experienced just the opposite. He saw the army with no commander. The prophet was surrounded by the entire Syrian army, who had all come to attack him. It is a full army against one person. Elisha's servant starts to panic. Elisha tells him not to worry because there are MORE on their side than against them. Then he prays for his servant to see what he already knows.

**2 Kings 6:17— "Lord, I pray, open his eyes that he may see." Then Yehovah opened the eyes of the young man, and he saw. And behold, the mountain was full of horses and chariots of fire all around Elisha.**

יְהוָה פְּקַח־נָא אֶת־עֵינָיו וְיִרְאֶה וַיִּפְקַח יְהוָה אֶת־עֵינֵי
הַנַּעַר וַיַּרְא וְהִנֵּה הָהָר מָלֵא סוּסִים וְרֶכֶב אֵשׁ סְבִיבֹת
אֱלִישָׁע׃

Here we have the army but no commander. Notice that the soldiers are angels, and that they have horses and chariots of fire. They are on the mountain top which seems to imply they have landed, after having come down from heaven. In Joshua 5 we have the Commander but no army. In 2 Kings 6 we have an army but no commander. Is there any place we see the army and the commander together? Yes.

**Revelation 19:11-14—Now I saw heaven open, and behold, a white horse. And He who sat on him was called Faithful and True, and in righteousness He judges and makes war. His eyes were like a flame of fire, and on His head were many crowns. He had a name written that no one knew except Himself. He was clothed with a robe dipped in blood, and His name is called The Word of God. And the armies in heaven, clothed in fine linen, white and clean, followed Him on white horses.**

Revelation 19 puts the army and the Commander together. It is the same army with horses and chariots of fire that have come out of heaven. The Commander is the same Commander. The connection between Revelation 19 and Joshua 5 is extremely significant. Revelation 19 demonstrates that the Commander of Joshua 5 is indeed Yeshua. The unity between these two images of the Divine Army Commander forms a profound connection between the world view of the New Covenant and the Old, between the Christian world view and the Jewish. When understood correctly, it is a bridge that provides a consistent theme from the beginning of Scriptures to the end.

In Joshua 5 we see the Commander, in 2 Kings 6 we see the army, in Revelation 19 we see the Commander and the army. Is there any

Bible passage that shows where the army is that they are coming to fight against? Where is the enemy? Where is the war? The prophet Zechariah gives the answer.

### Zechariah 14:1-2, 3-4, 5

**Behold, the day of Yehovah is coming, and your spoil will be divided in your midst. For I will gather all the nations to battle against Jerusalem; the city shall be taken...**

**Then Yehovah will go forth and fight against those nations, as He fights in the day of battle. And in that day His feet will stand on the Mount of Olives, which faces Jerusalem on the east...**

**Thus Yehovah my God will come, and all the saints with You.**

הִנֵּה יוֹם־בָּא לַיהוָה וְחֻלַּק שְׁלָלֵךְ בְּקִרְבֵּךְ: וְאָסַפְתִּי
אֶת־כָּל־הַגּוֹיִם אֶל־יְרוּשָׁלַ͏ִם לַמִּלְחָמָה וְנִלְכְּדָה הָעִיר
וְנָשַׁסּוּ הַבָּתִּים וְהַנָּשִׁים תִּשָּׁגַלְנָה וְיָצָא חֲצִי הָעִיר
בַּגּוֹלָה וְיֶתֶר הָעָם לֹא יִכָּרֵת מִן־הָעִיר: וְיָצָא יְהוָה
וְנִלְחַם בַּגּוֹיִם הָהֵם כְּיוֹם הִלָּחֲמוֹ בְּיוֹם קְרָב: וְעָמְדוּ
רַגְלָיו בַּיּוֹם־הַהוּא עַל־הַר הַזֵּיתִים אֲשֶׁר עַל־פְּנֵי
יְרוּשָׁלַ͏ִם מִקֶּדֶם וְנִבְקַע הַר הַזֵּיתִים מֵחֶצְיוֹ מִזְרָחָה וָיָמָּה
גֵּיא גְּדוֹלָה מְאֹד וּמָשׁ חֲצִי הָהָר צָפוֹנָה וְחֶצְיוֹ־נֶגְבָּה:
וּבָא יְהוָה אֱלֹהַי כָּל־קְדֹשִׁים עִמָּךְ:

The attack of the nations against Jerusalem is reiterated in Zechariah 12:3; 12:6; 12:9; 14:12 and 14:16. The Day of Yehovah referred to here is what is known in Christian circles as the Second Coming. The Israelite prophets referred to it as "the great and fearful day of Yehovah" (**Joel 1:15; 2:1; 2:11; 2:31; 3:14**). The great and fearful Day of Yehovah in Jewish thought and the Second Coming of Yeshua in Christian thought is the same event, the same time, the same Day.

**Zechariah 14:9**

**And Yehovah shall be king over all the earth. In that day it shall be—Yehovah is one and His name one.**

וְהָיָה יְהוָה לְמֶלֶךְ עַל־כָּל־הָאָרֶץ בַּיּוֹם הַהוּא יִהְיֶה יְהוָה אֶחָד וּשְׁמוֹ אֶחָד:

In that day, everything will come together into "one." Angel-Yehovah will not be artificially separated into the roles of covenant-maker of Abraham, law-giver of Moses, or army-commander of Joshua. He will fulfill all those roles together in one.

He will be King over all the earth. His kingdom will reign from Jerusalem over all the nations. There will be no more division between the remnant of Israel and the international Church. The Messianic kingdom will bring peace and prosperity on earth for 1,000 years.

In **Zechariah 14:4** above, notice that His feet will stand on the Mount of Olives. These are the same feet that stood on the Mount of Olives in **Acts 1:11-12**. As His feet lifted off from the Mount of Olives in Acts 1, so will they touch down again as in Zechariah 14. The word in Hebrew for feet רגליו in **Zechariah 14:4** is the same word found in **Exodus 24:10,** where the elders of Israel saw His feet and legs in a human-like form. The feet they saw on Mount Sinai will be seen again on the Mount of Olives. This same God-Man—whom we have seen in Genesis, Exodus, Joshua, Zechariah, Acts and Revelation—will come to fight the battles of the End Times and rule the earth from Jerusalem.

Revelation 19 and Zechariah 14 are the two clearest pictures of the Second Coming of Yeshua in the whole Bible. Revelation 19 gives the view from heaven; Zechariah 14 gives the view from earth. If we put the two pictures together, much of our understanding of the End Times will be clarified.

Seeing Yeshua as the Commander of the heavenly armies in both Revelation 19 and Joshua 5 gives great insight into His divinity and authority. Seeing the battle of Revelation 19 and Zechariah 14 as the same battle gives great insight into the Second Coming and the Millennium. (For a more complete study on this connection and on the End Times, see our book, *Iraq to Armageddon*, Destiny Image Press. The purpose of this present book is not an explanation of the End Times, but a comparison between Yeshua in the New Covenant and Angel-Yehovah in the Old Covenant.)

In this chapter we are seeking to understand Yeshua as an army commander. In Israel, all the young people serve in the army when they graduate from high school. All four of our children have done so. The armies of Israel are mentioned quite often in Scripture. There is a parallel between the armies of Israel on earth and the angelic armies of the God of Israel in heaven.

My oldest son, Heskel, serves as a captain in the Israeli army. He is a Spirit-filled, dedicated believer. He is married with a little baby daughter. He is very gentle on the inside. At the same time, because of his experience as an officer, he has a deep understanding of authority, of facing opposition, of standing firm before an enemy. He once told me, "If someone is coming to kill you, you have no option other than to remove from him the means to accomplish it." In Heskel, I see something of Yeshua that is both a gentle lamb and an army commander at the same time. I give this example in order to provide a little insight as to how Yeshua can have both gentle qualities and military qualities simultaneously.

In the ancient Israelite kingdom, there was a spiritual coordination between the angelic armies and the earthly armies. David would always pray before he went to battle in order to know whether the Lord wanted him to fight. The answer could be yes, or no. Then David would also pray to know when to fight and how to fight. David did not see himself as initiating any battles. He was submitting to the Lord's will. He left the decision and the direction up to the Lord.

One time the Lord told him to wait and listen for the sound of an army marching at the level of the tree tops just above him (**2 Sam. 5:23-25**). It was not that the angelic armies simply followed after David; he sought to follow after them. The spiritual army did more of the fighting than the earthly army. Yet there was a covenant connection between them.

David loved to worship the Lord in music and praise. Yet he also knew the Lord as an army commander. Many ask the Lord today to have a "heart like David." I agree. To have a Davidic heart, we must make worship and praise the first priority in our lives. Then we must have a tender heart of obedience and submission. In addition, we must know the Lord as the Commander-in-Chief. Not to know the military side of Yeshua is not to know Him.

Because Yeshua came to earth 2,000 years ago as a sacrificial lamb, many people today have difficulty relating to Him as an army commander. Yet it is only by seeing Yeshua as this army commander that we will be able to stand in the spiritual battles and tribulations of the End Times.

In recent years, the United Nations, the International Media and the Islamic Jihad have been fervent in attacking Israel. At the same time there are hundreds of Messianic Jewish boys and girls serving in the Israeli army. Because of the trend of current events and end times' prophecies, the revelation of Yeshua as the commander of the armies of the God of Israel is urgent and vital for Christians everywhere.

[Note: It is my hope that the revelation of Yeshua as Commander-in-Chief will help prepare the international Church for the End Times. The Holy Spirit has been continually impressing on my heart this urgent commission: **"Prepare the Church to stand with Israel in the events of the End Times leading up to the Second Coming of Yeshua."** If your heart confirms this word, please help share this exhortation with others.]

In **Joshua 5:14**, the Angel-Yehovah said that the issue is not whether He is on our side, but whether we are on His side. **Zechariah 14:3** states that He is coming to fight against all those who have come against Jerusalem. Many Jews want Jerusalem without Jesus. Many Christians want Jesus without Jerusalem. Secular Humanists and Islamic Jihadists stand in opposition to both. The question is not what we want, but what He wants. When He comes, will we be found fighting for Him, against Him, or just copping out?

# CHAPTER EIGHT
# *Who Fought the Battle of Jericho?*

When the divine army commander appeared to Joshua, notice that His sword was drawn in His hand. That means He was ready to fight.

**Joshua 5:13—And behold, a Man stood opposite him with His sword drawn in His hand.**

וְהִנֵּה־אִישׁ עֹמֵד לְנֶגְדּוֹ וְחַרְבּוֹ שְׁלוּפָה בְּיָדוֹ

We notice Angel-Yehovah in two other locations with His sword drawn. The next occasion was to Balaam on his donkey.

**Numbers 22:31—Then Yehovah opened Balaam's eyes, and he saw Angel-Yehovah standing in the way with His drawn sword in His hand; and he bowed down his head and fell flat on his face.**

וַיְגַל יְהוָה אֶת־עֵינֵי בִלְעָם וַיַּרְא אֶת־מַלְאַךְ יְהוָה נִצָּב
בַּדֶּרֶךְ וְחַרְבּוֹ שְׁלֻפָה בְּיָדוֹ וַיִּקֹּד וַיִּשְׁתַּחוּ לְאַפָּיו׃

Balaam was an independent "prophet" who had been hired by Balak king of Midian to curse the Jewish people in the wilderness. Angel-Yehovah stops him on the way to warn him that he must bless Israel and not curse them. At first glance God's treatment of Balaam seems a little harsh. But God saw an unseen evil in the hearts of Balak and Balaam.

After their attempts at sorcery against Israel failed, they turned to a planned program of sexual temptation, decadence and the occult.

**Numbers 25:1-2—Now Israel dwelt in Shittim and the people began to commit sexual immorality with the daughters of Moab. And those women called the people to make sacrifices to their gods; and the people ate and worshiped their gods.**

וַיֵּשֶׁב יִשְׂרָאֵל בַּשִּׁטִּים וַיָּחֶל הָעָם לִזְנוֹת אֶל־בְּנוֹת
מוֹאָב: וַתִּקְרֶאןָ לָעָם לִזְבְחֵי אֱלֹהֵיהֶן וַיֹּאכַל הָעָם
וַיִּשְׁתַּחֲווּ לֵאלֹהֵיהֶן:

The people of Israel were responsible for their own sin and were punished horribly (25,000 Israelites were killed). The complication with Midian resulted in a war in which tens of thousands of Midianites were killed as well. It was this disastrous situation that the Angel-Yehovah was warning about when He drew His sword.

[Note: This is a lesson learned throughout the Bible. Sometimes the Lord's punishments seem harsh to us. However, they are always just and gracious. He warns about problems in the present that He sees coming down the path in the future. His justice takes into account His foreknowledge. He sees that which we do not see. What we do know is that He is just and merciful, and that we can always trust Him.]

The Bible later clarifies that Balaam had an active part in planning the campaign of sexual immorality (**Num. 31:16**). He is seen as a false prophet in the New Covenant (**2 Pet. 2:15, Rev. 2:14**). He was killed in the war between Midian and Israel, a war which he was partly responsible for causing (**Num. 31:8**).

At a first reading one might question whether the angel with the sword drawn to Balaam was just an ordinary angel sent from God, or the divine Angel-Yehovah. The evidence for the divinity of this angel is three-fold:

1.  The paired-noun form (s'michut) of the name with Yehovah (**Num. 22:22, 24, 26, 27, 32, 34, 35**).

2.  The interchanging with the name Elohim or Yehovah (**Num. 22:9, 12, 13, 20, 22, 23, 28, 31, 35, 38**).

3.  The speaking to Balaam in first person authority as God throughout the passage (**Num. 22:20, 35, 38; 23:5**).

All these verses prove that this was not an ordinary angel that confronted Balaam but the divine Angel-Yehovah.

The third time we see the angel with the sword drawn is over the threshing floor of Araunah. In an act of egotism, King David had commanded a census of the people. Punishment in the form of a plague falls upon the nation. At the climax of the tension, David sees the Angel-Yehovah hovering in the air over Jerusalem.

**1 Chronicles 21:16—Then David lifted his eyes and saw Angel-Yehovah standing between earth and heaven, having in his hand a drawn sword stretched out over Jerusalem.**

וַיִּשָּׂא דָוִיד אֶת־עֵינָיו וַיַּרְא אֶת־מַלְאַךְ יְהוָה עֹמֵד בֵּין הָאָרֶץ וּבֵין הַשָּׁמַיִם וְחַרְבּוֹ שְׁלוּפָה בְּיָדוֹ נְטוּיָה עַל־יְרוּשָׁלָ͏ִם

Here we have the same paired-noun form of the name. However, in the rest of the passage, there is no other contextual evidence to indicate whether this angel is divine or a normal angel from among the ranks.

There is a parallel between Angel-Yehovah appearing here to David and the earlier appearance at the sacrifice of Isaac. They both occurred in the same location. In the first case, the sacrifice of Isaac was replaced with the ram. In the second case, the destruction of Jerusalem was halted in the middle. The dynamic tension between judgment and atonement are apparent in both situations.

Let's return to the battle of Jericho. Joshua was one of the greatest generals that ever lived. His encounter with the God-Man-Commander was on the eve of the Jericho battle. Before the battle, one important issue had to be settled. Were Joshua and Israel fighting on their own or were they submitted to the divine messenger?

As the leader of the tribes of Israel, Joshua submits 100 percent to the angelic Commander, and thus the blessing of God was secured. As any good leader the night before the battle, he was obviously concerned as to whether lives would be needlessly lost. Had the Commander told him not to fight, he would have agreed immediately to stop the battle. Once he had submitted, his concerns were settled, and he knew his people would have divine grace and protection.

Even though Joshua was a great military tactician, the battle was fought in a strange manner. Instead of attacking, the people went out and marched in silence around the city with the Ark of the Covenant. Just the shofars were sounded. This was not psychological warfare. This was spiritual warfare; an act of faith, of prayer and of praise. On the seventh day, with the sound of seven shofars, and a shout of victory, the walls of the city fell.

The question here is: who exactly fought this battle? The walls of the city fell without a single Israeli touching it. Yes, after the wall fell, they captured the city. However, it wouldn't take a military genius to win the battle after the walls collapse on top of enemy soldiers. Only secondary credit goes to Joshua. The primary battle was fought by the Commander of the angels and their heavenly army.

This victory reminds us of the "victory" of Yehoshaphat over the Ammonites and the Moabites (**2 Chron. 20**). He received a prophecy saying that he did not need to fight the battle. The Lord Himself would do the fighting (**v. 15**). All they had to do was stand there and believe (**v. 17**). The people went out with musical instruments and began to praise the Lord in front of their enemies (**v. 21**). As soon as they began to praise the Lord in song, God brought a supernatural victory over their enemies (**v. 22**).

The people did not do the essential part of the fighting. The one who fought the battles was the Commander of the Army of Yehovah, along with all His warrior angels. Spiritual warfare is not military war alone. Nor is it spirituality disconnected from a military situation. Spiritual warfare is the connection between the heavenly armies and the earthly ones. Our prayers, prophecies and praise affect angels, who in turn, affect the military, economic and political situation around us.

[For this reason our staff dedicates almost two hours every weekday morning for "watches" of prayer, prophecy and praise. We believe that what we do in the spirit affects the world around us.]

Another example of divine intervention in military warfare was during the attack of Assyrian king Sennacherib on Jerusalem. Israel is greatly outnumbered. Hezekiah and Isaiah lead the people in prayer and fasting. Here is the outcome:

**Isaiah 37:36—Then Angel-Yehovah went out, and killed in the camp of the Assyrians one hundred and eighty-five thousand; and when people arose early in the morning, there were corpses—all dead.**

וַיֵּצֵא מַלְאַךְ יְהוָה וַיַּכֶּה בְּמַחֲנֵה אַשּׁוּר מֵאָה וּשְׁמֹנִים וַחֲמִשָּׁה אָלֶף וַיַּשְׁכִּימוּ בַבֹּקֶר וְהִנֵּה כֻלָּם פְּגָרִים מֵתִים:

This is an enormous number—185,000 people in one night! The passage does not give any extra details. Were there other angels or just one? If it was just one, was it the divine Angel-Yehovah, or not? If so, was this actually Yeshua Himself? Killing 185,000 enemy soldiers in one night might be hard for us to reconcile with the image of Yeshua. Yet, the book of Revelation describes wars with much greater casualties than this. Those wars involve the direct intervention of Yeshua Himself (**Rev. 9:15-18; 15:19-20; 19:11-16**).

[**Note:** Seeing the connection in the book of Revelation between praise and worship on the one hand and the battles of the tribulation on the other is an important key for the Church to understand spiritual warfare in the end times.]

When we read about such large numbers, the prophecies might seem impossible. Yet with the increase of millions of people to the ranks of Islamic Jihad, and with the bizarre advocacy of Jihad by the news media and the United Nations, the coming of a world-wide holocaust in the not very distant future seems not only possible but unavoidable.

The Angel-Yehovah and His angelic armies did most of the work in helping Joshua's generation take possession of the land of Canaan. Their work continued through the time of the Judges as well.

**Judges 2:1—Then Angel-Yehovah came up from Gilgal to Bochim, and said: "I led you up from Egypt and brought you**

**to the land which I swore to your fathers; and I said, 'I will never break My covenant with you...'"**

וַיַּעַל מַלְאַדְ־יְהוָה מִן־הַגִּלְגָּל אֶל־הַבֹּכִים פ וַיֹּאמֶר
אַעֲלֶה אֶתְכֶם מִמִּצְרַיִם וָאָבִיא אֶתְכֶם אֶל־הָאָרֶץ אֲשֶׁר
נִשְׁבַּעְתִּי לַאֲבֹתֵיכֶם וָאֹמַר לֹא־אָפֵר בְּרִיתִי אִתְּכֶם
לְעוֹלָם:

In this one verse, the Angel speaks as God in the first person five times. The word "angel" מלאך —*mal'ach* comes from an Arabic root meaning "to send." (It is not much different from the idea of an apostle as a "sent one.") The Angel here was sent from Yehovah. At the same time He speaks as God in the first person. How can He be sent from God and be divine at the same time? That is the mystery of this same figure that we see throughout the Law and Prophets.

This dual nature—being sent from God and yet being God—is consistent with the descriptions of Yeshua in the New Covenant. There should be perfect consistency on this issue between the ancient Israelite prophets and any modern day Christian.

In the **Judges 2** passage, the Angel claims to be the one who 1) cut covenant with the patriarchs, 2) brought Israel out of Egypt, and 3) led them into the land of Canaan. To understand the implications of this verse, try inserting Yeshua into the picture. Yeshua was the divine Angel who cut covenant with Abraham, split the Red Sea, and fought the battle of Jericho. That picture is rather startling to both Jewish and Christian understanding of the Bible.

Angel-Yehovah also appeared to Gideon. This time instead of coming with a sword drawn, He simply sat down in the shade under a tree across from where Gideon was working, threshing the wheat.

**Judges 6:12—And Angel-Yehovah appeared to him, and said to him, "Yehovah is with you, you mighty man of valor!"**

וַיֵּרָא אֵלָיו מַלְאַדְ יְהוָה וַיֹּאמֶר אֵלָיו יְהוָה עִמְּךָ גִּבּוֹר
הֶחָיִל:

This was not some passerby who called him a mighty soldier, but the Commander of the armies of Yehovah. The Commander challenges Gideon to go out and fight the Midianites, and promises to accompany him on this military campaign (**v. 16**).

**Judges 6:14—Then Yehovah turned to him and said, "Go in this might of yours, and you shall save Israel from the hand of Midianites. Have I not sent you."**

וַיִּפֶן אֵלָיו יְהוָה וַיֹּאמֶר לֵךְ בְּכֹחֲךָ זֶה וְהוֹשַׁעְתָּ
אֶת־יִשְׂרָאֵל מִכַּף מִדְיָן הֲלֹא שְׁלַחְתִּיךָ:

In this one chapter, the divine messenger is referred to seven times as "angel" (**vv. 11, 12, 20, 21, 21, 22, 22**). He is referred to directly as Yehovah five times (**vv. 12, 14, 16, 22, 23**); and as Adonai twice (**vv. 15, 22**). Throughout the whole passage, He speaks in the first person with divine authority. Again we have the inescapable conclusion that this figure is sent from God, and yet at the same time is God.

Our last example in this section is the appearance to Manoah and his wife, the parents of Samson.

**Judges 13:3—And Angel-Yehovah appeared to the woman...**

וַיֵּרָא מַלְאַךְ־יְהוָה אֶל־הָאִשָּׁה...

The passage is a variant of the same pattern, another in the series of angelic visitations. The divine messenger appears first to Manoah's wife, and then a second time to both of them. He predicts the upcoming birth of Samson (reminiscent of the prophecy to Sarah in **Gen. 18** by the same visitor).

The visitor is referred to as a man five times, as Angel-Yehovah ten times, and as God (Elohim) one time (**v. 22**). He is never referred to as just "angel." In **verse 17**, Manoah asks Him what His name is, and He refuses (similar to His refusal to answer Jacob when he asked the same question in **Gen. 32:29**), this time saying that His name is wondrous (פלאי —*Peleh*). This word "wondrous" is the same word used in the prophecy about the name of the Messiah in **Isaiah 9:5**.

Similar to the encounter with Gideon, the Angel-Yehovah leaves supernaturally as the flame of the meat offering rises (**Judg. 6:21; 13:20**). As Angel-Yehovah leaves, Manoah cries out that he is afraid they will die because they have seen God (**v. 22**). This indicates they were familiar with the story of the encounter between Moses and Angel-Yehovah in **Exodus 33**. They were convinced that they saw God.

All the appearances of Angel-Yehovah to the people of Israel in the time of Joshua and Judges were perfectly consistent with the appearances throughout the Torah. The additional revelation in these passages, not previously seen, is His role as the Commander of the armies, and the fact that it was He who led the conquest of Canaan.

Even if one does not see Yeshua in this figure, it is undeniable that the central figure of the Tanakh is this divine messenger, who is at one and the same time God, an Angel and a Man. He was the center of the faith of the Israelite prophets and patriarchs. [For a discussion of this figure among the ancient Israelites in document criticism, see Appendix #2, "The Divine Angel," by Solomon Intrater.]

# CHAPTER NINE
## Possessing the Land

Yeshua's **position** in this section is the Commander of the Armies of Yehovah. His **purpose** was to take possession of the land of Canaan. We want to address briefly the purpose of "taking the land" in this chapter.

One of the core values of the Jewish people is a love for the land of Israel. There is a revelation about the land of Israel that is unknown to most of the Church. Yet, this revelation has enormous importance for Christians everywhere and greatly affects the Christian worldview of the kingdom of God.

When God looks at the human race, He sees a family of nations. Each ethnic and language group is its own family (**Rev. 7:9; 17:15**). God loves all of them equally. Israel is considered to be the first born among the nations, primarily because Abraham was the first believer to raise his family under the covenant (**Exod. 4:22; Gen. 18:19**).

As the first born, Israel becomes a "pattern nation" for the nations of the world. What is true for her is true for others. What happens to Israel in the Bible is a specific history in time and space. However, their history becomes a universal principle for all nations in their own geographic location and historical development. [There is a rabbinic principle of biblical interpretation called *klal v'prat, prat v'klal* — כלל ופרט, פרט וכלל. The general becomes the specific, and the specific becomes the general.]

Each of the nations of the world was given a mandate to take possession of their own land in their own borders according to the pattern set by the children of Israel.

**Deuteronomy 32:8—When the Most High divided their inheritance to the nations, when He separated the sons of Adam, He set the borders of the peoples according to the number of the children of Israel.**

בְּהַנְחֵל עֶלְיוֹן גּוֹיִם בְּהַפְרִידוֹ בְּנֵי אָדָם יַצֵּב גְּבֻלֹת עַמִּים
לְמִסְפַּר בְּנֵי יִשְׂרָאֵל:

The principle of God giving every nation a dwelling place is repeated in Saul's (Paul's) address on Mars Hill.

**Acts 17:26—And He has made from one blood every nation of men to dwell on the face of the earth, and has determined their pre-appointed times and the boundaries of their dwellings.**

Israel is the pattern for the nations. According to the pattern, each nation is given their own inheritance, a land to take possession of for themselves. As Israel was called to take possession of the Land of Promise, so is the international Church called to take possession of the Planet Earth.

The Bible speaks of patterns of judgment, exile and restoration, similar to what happened to Israel, for other nations, such as Babylon (**Jer. 12:15**), Moab (**Jer. 48:47**), Ammon (**Jer. 49:6**), Elam (**Jer. 49:39**), Egypt (**Ezek. 29:12-14**) and Ethiopia (**Amos 9:7**). What happened to Israel is applicable to the Church as well. As Israel had a Levitical priesthood, so is there a priesthood of all Christian believers in their own nations and cultures.

A major portion of the Hebrew Scriptures deals with the mandate of "taking possession of the land." The very first word that God said to Abraham—the first believer, and the first "Israelite" —was to go to the land of Israel and take possession by faith (**Gen. 12:1**). Over and over again, God made an eternal, unbreakable covenant promise to our forefathers to give them the land of Israel as an inheritance (**Gen. 12:7; 13:15; 15:7; 24:7; 26:3; 28:4; 28:13; 35:12; 48:4**). [For a more detailed study on the topic, see our booklet **"What Does the Bible Really Say about the Land?"**]

The Israelites primarily lived as "pilgrims" in that land. The fullness of the land-possession promises had never taken place, and still has not. However, the lack of total fulfillment did not affect the eternal purpose of God. The possession of the land is an issue of covenant and faith. Part of the promises will be fulfilled now, and part will be fulfilled in the Millennial kingdom.

**Hebrews 11:8-9**—By faith Abraham obeyed when he was called to go out to the place which he would receive as an inheritance in the future. And he went out, not knowing where he was going. By faith he dwelt in the land of promise as a sojourner in a foreign land, dwelling in tents with Isaac and Jacob, the heir with him of the same promise.

When the children of Jacob were exiled to Egypt, they yearned to come back to the Promised Land. Jacob made Joseph promise to bury him there. And Joseph made his sons promise to take his bones up from Egypt at the time of deliverance. It was obvious to them that their descendants would return, no matter how long it took. After all, God had made an unbreakable covenant with them. The oath to have their dead bodies buried there showed that they knew the final fulfillment of the land promises would take place at the time of the resurrection.

The issue of the kingdom of God being fulfilled on earth through possession of the land of Israel is such a central issue of the Scriptures that it becomes almost an obsession with the people of God. Moses took the people of Israel out of Egypt in order to take them back to the Promised Land. Moses had a heated argument with God, pleading with Him in a heart-rending fashion, to let him enter the land before he died (**Deut. 4:23-27**).

All of the judges and generals, kings and prophets, fought for the right to stay in the land of Israel. Jeremiah and Ezekiel, who prophesied the exile from the land, also prophesied the restoration to the land. A further wave of possessing the land took place at the end of the Old Covenant with the books of Ezra and Nehemiah. (The yearning of the Jewish people for the Promised Land is parallel to the Christian yearning for heaven. Ultimately those two world views must come together into one, like body and soul.)

In **Luke 21:24,** Yeshua prophesies that the people of Israel would **"fall by the edge of the sword, and be led away captive to all nations."** Yeshua declared this prophecy in 33 A.D. In 70 A.D. the prophecy came to pass. He predicted the destruction of Jerusalem and the great exile. Yet, in the same verse Yeshua said **"Jerusalem will be trampled underfoot by the Gentiles until**

**the times of the Gentiles are fulfilled."** The destruction and exile would take place **"until"** a future specific time.

This indicates a time of completion for the punishment, and therefore a restoration to follow. One day Jerusalem would not be trampled underfoot by Gentiles, which indicates that it would be re-inhabited by Jews. Jerusalem was recaptured by the Jews in 1967. The recapture of Jerusalem was an initial stage of fulfillment of this verse and of the many other verses that speak of Jerusalem's restoration.

In **Acts 1:6**, Yeshua's disciples asked Him if He would at that time **"restore the kingdom to Israel."** Yeshua did not say "No," but told them that they cannot know when it will take place. In saying that the date is unknown, He was clearly affirming that the event would one day take place. The nation of Israel goes through a process of destruction and restoration that is parallel to the death and resurrection of Yeshua.

So what does this mean for the international Church? What is true for Abraham's tribal family is also true for Abraham's greater spiritual family. Ultimately, the international Church, with the believing remnant of Israel, will inherit all of planet earth. Unfortunately, here is where many Christians hit a stumbling block and blind spot in their faith.

Abraham was not called to inherit just one small piece of real estate in the Middle East. His "seed" was called to inherit planet earth; to take back what Adam had lost to the devil.

**Romans 4:13—For the promise that he would be the heir of the world was not given to Abraham or his seed on the basis of the Torah, but on the basis of righteousness that he obtained by faith.**

What was the promise made to Abraham? What was he to inherit by faith? It was not just to die and go to heaven. Nor was it just the tiny land of Canaan. He was called to inherit the whole world, and all of the real estate in it. How was he to obtain this inheritance? By faith. And who was to inherit it with him? All of his "seed," those who have like faith as Abraham.

Abraham's spiritual children are those who have faith in Yeshua as Messiah. They will inherit together with him if they have faith like him. Do you have faith to inherit this planet together with Abraham? Or has false ("pie in the sky"— "helicopter ticket"— "fire insurance") theology made you receive only the spiritual part of your inheritance and not the earthly part?

Please don't misunderstand. I believe in all the heavenly spiritual promises just as all Christians do. But I believe there are earthly promises as well as heavenly. The kingdom of God involves a harmony of the earthly and the spiritual. Taking just the spiritual part without the natural part is not biblical Christianity; it is a Christianized form of Hinduism. If all the promises of God were heavenly only, why would you need a resurrection body? You can go to heaven when you die without ever being resurrected. The promise of a resurrected body demands a restoration of planet earth.

**Romans 8:19-22**

**For the earnest expectation of the creation eagerly waits for the revealing of the sons of God. The creation was subjected to futility, not willingly, but of the One who subjected it in hope. Creation itself will also be delivered from the bondage of corruption into the glorious liberty of the children of God. For we know that all the creation groans and labors with birth pangs until this very day.**

Please re-read these verses. I can almost feel creation groaning as you start to grasp this revelation. Part of the plan of salvation includes planet earth. In Yeshua, God will restore everything that was stolen. We believe in total restoration. Not only will Israel be restored (**"Will You at this time restore the kingdom to Israel? [Acts 1:6]; "What will their restoration be?"[Rom. 11:15]**, but so will all things promised in the Bible be restored.) (**"Elijah is coming first and will restore all things" [Matt. 17:11]; "Until the times of the restoration of all things" [Acts 3:21]**).

This total restoration includes everything promised by the ancient Israelite prophets, starting from the book of Genesis. Biblical restoration includes the regeneration of planet earth.

**Matthew 19:28—So Yeshua said to them, "Assuredly I say to you, that when creation is renewed, when the Son of Man sits on the throne of His glory, you who have followed Me will also sit on twelve thrones, judging the twelve tribes of Israel.**

The renewal of creation is called "regeneration." Yeshua will return to rule and reign. Creation will be restored. Those who are righteous and have served Him loyally will rule in His government on this planet. Those righteous will not be only from the twelve tribes of Israel (**Rev. 7:4**), but will include an innumerable multitude from every nation, tribe and tongue (**Rev. 7:9**). I'm sure you would like to take part in this.

Jewish thought has a concept called *Tikkun Olam*—תיקון עולם; restoring or repairing the world. It is a biblical concept. It is repeated every day in the Jewish prayer book in the hymn called "Aleinu"—עלינו—"It is incumbent upon us." The prayer calls for the fulfillment of the hope that God will "repair the world in the kingdom of El Shaddai." The prayers of all true Bible believers should be for the world to be repaired and restored according to God's plan. [For a further explanation, see Appendix # 7, on "Restoration of All Things."]

God's plan involves both heaven and earth, not just heaven. He created heaven and earth together in the beginning (**Gen. 1:1**), and everything God created was "very good" (**Gen. 1:31**). God delegated the earth into the hands of man (**Ps. 115:16**). We, of course, have made a mess of things ever since, because of our sin. Inherent in the forgiveness of our sin is God's promise to renew and redeem what we have destroyed on this planet. The earth will be restored in a new creation (**Isa. 65:17; 2 Pet. 3:5-12; Rev. 21-22**).

**Matthew 5:3, 5—Blessed are the poor in spirit, for theirs is the kingdom of heaven. Blessed are the meek, for they shall inherit the earth.**

The earth is to be inherited by the saints, not the sinners. Yeshua will return; Satan will be removed; the righteous will be resurrected; and the meek will inherit the earth. When Yeshua said that the meek will inherit the earth, He expanded the covenant promise to Abraham, by making it available to all of Abraham's spiritual children by faith.

Our prayers are not to abandon this planet (**John 17:15**). We were taught to pray that God's will would be done on earth as it is in heaven (**Matt. 6:10**). The final stage of God's plan is to bring everything together into unity and harmony—what is in heaven and what is on earth through Yeshua the Messiah (**Eph. 1:10; Col. 1:16; Zech. 14:9**). Yeshua has been given all authority, not just in heaven, but also on earth (**Matt. 28:18**). Our faith should be directed toward taking over, not running away. You are called to inherit the earth. [For a further explanation, see Appendix #8 on "Heaven and Earth."]

Earlier I mentioned that the most important construct I ever learned in Hebrew grammar was the paired-noun "s'michut" form. Now I want to tell you the most important word I ever learned in Hebrew vocabulary. The word is *aretz*—ארץ. Arets has TWO meanings. The first meaning is the "land of Israel"; the second meaning is "planet earth." The two-fold meaning of the word aretz makes for a two-fold fulfillment concerning the covenant promises about the "land."

Are the promises just for the land of Israel or do they pertain to the whole earth? Are the promises just for the remnant of Israel or do they pertain to the true international Church? The answer is both. What is true for the patriarchs and prophets in the land of Israel is true for the Church in all of planet earth.

This is a profound revelation. You are not a disembodied spirit. You are an earthly dwelling place for God. You were created as a three dimensional creature: spirit, soul and body. God created the universe with both heaven and earth. The covenant promises to Abraham to inherit the land are relevant for true believers in whatever land they live in. This holds true for the present life and the world to come.

In the battle at Ziklag, God told David he would recover everything he had lost (**1 Sam. 30:8, 18**). David believed and received. We have the heart of David today to recover everything that the human race lost to sin and Satan. That includes all of planet earth and the fullness thereof (**Ps. 24:1**). Wake up, dear saints.

The land of Israel is for the people of Israel. Every nation has been given a place to live as well. In the resurrection, the world will be inherited by the meek of every nation. The true Church is the extension of the righteous remnant of Israel. What the Messianic remnant of Israel has in inheritance toward the land of Israel, so does the righteous Christian remnant of every other nation have for their own land.

As passionate as the people of Israel are for the restoration of the land of Israel, so should every Christian be passionate about the restoration of his own nation, of Israel, and of planet earth. Since the promises to the Church are an extension of the promises made to Israel; and since Israel is the "firstborn son" of the family of nations; the promises need to be fulfilled in sequence to Israel first. If the promises of inheritance and restoration are not true for Israel, then they are not valid for the Church either.

In the possession of the land of Canaan, there were two types of inheritance. One was within the land of Israel, and the other was outside the borders of Israel. Some of the tribes chose to take their inheritance on the other side of the Jordan. That was perfectly acceptable to God on one condition. They had to help those inheriting within Israel to come into their possession first. Then they would be allowed by covenant to take possession of their own lands. (Please read the full account in **Num. 32:20-30**.) This story is a model for understanding the relationship between Israel and the Church; and to understand our mutual covenant mandate to take possession of planet earth.

Let's return to the subject of the Angel-Yehovah in the book of Joshua. Can we fathom that it was Yeshua who led the conquest of the land of Israel over 3,000 years ago? This is not an issue of culture or racism or politics. Yeshua led that conquest to lay the foundations for the future coming of the kingdom of God. Through the conquest of Canaan, Yeshua was laying claim that the earth belongs to God, that God's will would eventually be done on earth as it is in heaven, and that the planet would be given as an inheritance to godly believers by covenant.

The conquest of the land of Canaan was so central to the kingdom of God back then, that Yeshua Himself, as Angel-Yehovah, led the military campaign that took the land. He fulfilled the first stage of the covenant promise He made to Abraham. The Angel-Yehovah promised the land of Canaan to Abraham and his descendants. Almost 1,000 years after His promise to Abraham, He led the children of Israel to take possession of that land.

This viewpoint stretches the worldviews on both the Christian and Jewish sides. As the Angel-Yehovah, Yeshua Himself was the first "Zionist." Here I am speaking of Zionism in its purest biblical sense as the restoration of the Jewish people to the land of Canaan. (It is not within the scope or purpose of this book to deal with the relationship between the current political state of Israel and the prophetic promises of restoration.)

God's purpose goes beyond Zionism. The ultimate goal is that the children of God take part in the redemption of this planet and all that is in it, reclaiming it for the original purposes that God intended. That goal is worth fighting for.

Yeshua appeared before Joshua with His sword drawn (**Josh. 5:13**). From a spiritual viewpoint, Yeshua has a two-edged sword that proceeds from His mouth (**Rev. 1:16; 2:12; 19:15**). The battle is partially with military might, but even more so in words (particularly in the light of modern telecommunication). Actually, so was it back then as well. Even in the time of Joshua, the weapons were more spiritual than earthly (**2 Cor. 10:3-5; Eph. 6:10-19**).

In recent wars and security confrontations, whether in Lebanon against Hezbollah or in Gaza against Hamas, Israel has been morally justified (in my opinion) in the military actions it has taken. However, in every case, world public opinion was twisted through bizarre media spins and Jihadist propaganda. The battle has only partially to do with military weaponry. Both in the past as well as today, the battle is a spiritual one between truth and falsehood.

We are to continue the spiritual battle that Joshua started. The spiritual warfare takes precedence over the military part. As it was with Joshua, so is it with us: Angel-Yehovah led him in the battle; all Joshua had to do was submit to that Commander. Today the root issue is not just who has the right to the land of Israel, but whether the God of Israel has ownership rights to this entire planet.

I am not asking you to join the army of Israel. I am asking you to pray about what the spiritual meaning of the book of Joshua is for us today. When we see Yeshua as the Angel-Yehovah-Commander who led the armies in the conquest of Canaan, we will see the kingdom of God and the current political situation in a much different light.

Doesn't it seem strange that left-wing extremists are often so supportive of oppressive Islamic regimes? How could that be? The answer is that there is a spiritual battle behind the scenes; a battle which includes angelic and demonic powers and principalities. Ultimately the fight is against the authority of God and His Messiah to rule upon this planet (**Ps. 2:1-6**). Yeshua is the Messiah, head of the Church and the king of Israel.

God gave this planet to Adam in the beginning. Adam yielded it to Satan. Yeshua came to redeem both us and the planet. Satan is fighting against losing his control of the world systems on this earth. Thank God, Yeshua wins; Satan will be removed and punished eternally. It is time for the saints to stand in faith.

**Joshua 1:5-6—No man shall be able to stand before you all the days of your life; as I was with Moses, so will I be with you. I will not leave you nor forsake you. Be strong and very courageous, for to this people you shall cause this people to take possession of the land that I swore to your forefathers to give to them.**

לֹא־יִתְיַצֵּב אִישׁ לְפָנֶיךָ כֹּל יְמֵי חַיֶּיךָ כַּאֲשֶׁר הָיִיתִי
עִם־מֹשֶׁה אֶהְיֶה עִמָּךְ לֹא אַרְפְּךָ וְלֹא אֶעֶזְבֶךָּ: חֲזַק וֶאֱמָץ
כִּי אַתָּה תַּנְחִיל אֶת־הָעָם הַזֶּה אֶת־הָאָרֶץ
אֲשֶׁר־נִשְׁבַּעְתִּי לַאֲבוֹתָם לָתֵת לָהֶם:

I want these verses to come alive to you today. Place yourself in the passage. It is not just referring to the land of Canaan 3,000 years ago. It is speaking to us right now. It is speaking of the whole planet earth.

I hear the Holy Spirit emphasizing in my heart over and over again what He said to Joshua: **"You will cause My people to inherit the land."** Can you hear that as well? Let us take up the mandate for **"God's people to inherit planet earth."** We need to be strong by the word of God and by the Spirit of God. All the forces of evil stand in opposition to God's claim that this planet belongs to Him. God will take the earth away from the evil and give it to the righteous.

Yeshua is God's Commander given charge to accomplish this mission. You and I are His servants, His co-workers. What Yeshua did 3,000 years ago for Joshua's generation as they took possession of Canaan, so will He do for all His saints to take possession of planet earth at His Second Coming.

The name Yeshua and Joshua are the same name at root. Sometimes I think it is unfortunate that Yeshua's name did not become as popular as "Joshua" instead of "Jesus." Yeshua was given His name for TWO reasons. First, because it means, "God will save." Yeshua came the first time to save us of our sins (**Matt. 1:21; 18:12; Luke 19:10**). However, Yeshua was given this name for another reason. The name should make a mental association between Jesus (Yeshua) and Joshua (Yehoshua). Yeshua will come again soon. He will come in the image of Joshua.

The book of Joshua is a true historical account; yet it also serves as a prophetic parable for this generation of the end times. As the Angel-Yehovah led Joshua into victory to take the land, Yeshua will lead God's children everywhere to inherit the earth and take possession of the land. The righteous will take possession of the earth as the Israelites took possession of the land of Canaan. Yeshua was given the same name as Joshua to show us that Yeshua will take possession of planet earth at the Second Coming.

# PART FOUR

# The Prophets

In this section, we examine the appearances of God to the prophets in Israel and in the Exile.

In this period we discover the fullness of the glory of God. We find the God-Man in the fullness of that glory...

We will also analyze why the manifestation of God to mankind had to come through someone who was a man himself. We will show how the authority of the kingdom of God was transferred from our Heavenly Father to one who is the Son of Man.

# CHAPTER TEN
## Who is Sitting in the Chair?

One of the most amazing examples of God's appearing in the form of a man is found in Ezekiel chapter one. In Christian circles it is known as the description of the "Glory of the Lord." In Jewish circles it is known as "The Chariot." The ramifications of this passage are so "dangerous" that there is actually a rabbinic warning against reading it.

[In the Babylonian Talmud, Tractate "Chagigah," folio 14, side B warns even against a sage reading this chapter alone. It also tells a story of four rabbis who studied it in depth. One died, one went crazy, and one became an apostate (a Christian). Only Rabbi Akiva succeeded in surviving unharmed.]

**Ezekiel 1:1—Now it came to pass in the thirtieth year, in the fourth month, on the fifth day of the month, as I was among the captives by the River Chebar, that the heavens were opened and I saw appearances of God.**

וַיְהִי בִּשְׁלֹשִׁים שָׁנָה בָּרְבִיעִי בַּחֲמִשָּׁה לַחֹדֶשׁ וַאֲנִי
בְתוֹךְ־הַגּוֹלָה עַל־נְהַר־כְּבָר נִפְתְּחוּ הַשָּׁמַיִם וָאֶרְאֶה
מַרְאוֹת אֱלֹהִים:

As happened several times to the apostle John in the book of Revelation, the heavens suddenly were opened. Ezekiel saw God directly. This kind of exposure to the full glory of God could have killed a man, but because it was more a vision than a visitation, Ezekiel's life was preserved.

Ezekiel had an open vision. This means that he did not just have an inner picture of something from the spiritual realm. Here the "heavens were opened." To that point in history, this was the greatest vision anyone had ever had of the glory of God. There is much of creation that we do not see. Ezekiel saw into that world.

The creation is divided into two halves, or two dimensions. One is visible and the other is not visible (**Col. 1:15-16**). The part that we cannot see is the spiritual. The part that we can see is the physical. Yet, the invisible spiritual part is just as real and corporeal as the physical part. The fact that we cannot see it does not mean that it is not there. Both operate according to laws, physical and spiritual. The invisible part was created first and the visible part was created from and out of the invisible part (**Heb. 11:3**).

That we do not see the unseen part of creation does not mean that it cannot be seen. It is unseen to us but it is not "un-seeable." Under normal circumstances we ought to be able to see both dimensions. Before Adam and Eve sinned, they were able to see both. At the time they sinned, their sight became restricted. It was as if a barrier was placed between the seen and the unseen realm in order to prevent us from seeing the spiritual part.

The barrier between the physical and the spiritual, the seen and the unseen, is symbolized in the Temple by the great veil (*parochet* in Hebrew—פרוכת). That veil was torn in two by God when Yeshua was crucified (**Matt. 27:51**). That tearing symbolized the fact that a new way had been made available for access from the physical world of men to the spiritual world of God and the angels.

That barrier is more internal than it is external. The barrier is a limitation on human eyes. It is not so much a limitation on our physical eyes as it is a limitation on our spiritual eyes, the eyes of our heart (**Eph. 1:16**). The veil in the Temple matched a spiritual veil on our hearts. When anyone turns to Yeshua in faith, that veil begins to be removed (**2 Cor 3:16**). Until one is born again, he cannot see the spiritual world (kingdom of God). However, with the new birth comes a potential to see the things of the spirit (**John 3:3**).

From time to time during the period of the Hebrew prophets, the anointing of the Holy Spirit would come upon one of them and allow them to see into that spiritual world. This was called a vision or a revelation. This is what Ezekiel saw. A vision is the momentary experience of someone in the physical realm to see what is in the spiritual realm. The experience would be similar to someone receiving special glasses that would allow him to see infrared or ultraviolet rays, or to see radio or television waves. Those elements outside our natural perception were there all along; at a moment of special "seeing," we would be able to perceive them.

The most extended vision that anyone ever experienced was John (Yochanan), and we call that the "Book of Revelation" (**Rev. 1:1**). His revelation was simply a wider and fuller view of the same elements of the spiritual world that the ancient prophets already had glimpses of.

The laws of time and space operate somewhat differently in the spiritual realm, but they do operate according to rules. "Quantum" physics operate by different laws than the average person is aware of. Yet those laws exist and operate just as consistently as the laws of gravity. The laws of relativity, discovered by Einstein, show that time, mass and volume all change when matter approaches the speed of light.

From time to time men could see into the spiritual dimension of creation. At other times beings from that world would come to visit in our world. The first is called a vision; the second is a visitation. Angels are beings from the invisible dimension.

**Ezekiel 1:4—Then I looked, and behold, a whirlwind was coming out of the north, a great cloud with raging fire engulfing itself; and brightness was all around it and radiating out of it, like electric flashes in the midst of the fire.**

וָאֵרֶא וְהִנֵּה רוּחַ סְעָרָה בָּאָה מִן־הַצָּפוֹן עָנָן גָּדוֹל וְאֵשׁ מִתְלַקַּחַת וְנֹגַהּ לוֹ סָבִיב וּמִתּוֹכָהּ כְּעֵין הַחַשְׁמַל מִתּוֹךְ הָאֵשׁ:

This was the same glory power that came down on Mount Sinai and made the whole surrounding area tremble. Ezekiel goes on to describe four terrifying creatures with wings and faces of a man, a lion, an ox and an eagle. Lightning is shooting out of the whirlwind. He describes wheels within wheels. All these form a giant pillar that reaches from the ground to the sky.

The closest thing we could imagine to this would be the mushroom cloud of a nuclear explosion. Ezekiel did his best to describe in words of 3,000 years ago a pillar of nuclear-like power.

**Ezekiel 1:22—The likeness of the firmament above the heads of the living creatures was, like the color of an awesome crystal, stretched out over their heads.**

וּדְמוּת עַל־רָאשֵׁי הַחַיָּה רָקִיעַ כְּעֵין הַקֶּרַח הַנּוֹרָא נָטוּי עַל־רָאשֵׁיהֶם מִלְמָעְלָה:

The book of Genesis states that God created the world with a firmament between heaven and earth. Until this time no one had ever seen it. The root of the word firmament means a surface that someone could stand on. According to Ezekiel's description, there is a spiritual surface, relatively transparent, that stretches over our heads, like the ceiling of a lower apartment that becomes the flooring of the upper apartment. It is obviously made of a material or energy substance that we do not have on this earth.

The "nuclear" pillar of the glory of God in Ezekiel's vision stretched from the ground to that firmament ceiling-flooring. All this is leading up to what Ezekiel saw next. His eyes began to move upward in astonishment as he looked at the glory cloud. His eyes reached the firmament. Since the firmament is transparent, he looked at what is above the firmament, over the heads of the terrifying creatures.

Despite all the shocking elements of what he has seen of the glory cloud, what he saw next was the greatest shock of all.

**Ezekiel 1:26—And above the firmament over their heads was the likeness of a throne, in appearance like a sapphire stone; on the likeness of the throne was a likeness with the appearance of a man on it from above.**

וּמִמַּעַל לָרָקִיעַ אֲשֶׁר עַל־רֹאשָׁם כְּמַרְאֵה כִּסֵּא וְעַל דְּמוּת הַכִּסֵּא דְּמוּת כְּמַרְאֵה אָדָם עָלָיו מִלְמָעְלָה:

He saw a chair.

(The word for throne in Hebrew is the same as the word for chair—כיסא.) This was a throne, a chair, a place for someone to sit. This was no ordinary throne. It was a brilliant, radiating jewel-like throne. But even more important was what he saw on the chair.

On the chair he saw a man. He saw a Man. He saw a supernatural being in the likeness of a man.

(The word "likeness" of a man, immediately reminds us that man was created in the likeness of God. Ezekiel said this supernatural figure was in the likeness of a man. Perhaps we could say in retrospect, we men are made in the likeness of this Man.)

In the very center of this vision, sitting on top of the nuclear cloud, on a radiant jewel-like throne above the cherubim and above the firmament—is a Man, or more exactly, one in the appearance of a man.

**Ezekiel 1:27—Also from the appearance of his waist and upward I saw, as it were, like fire with electric flashes inside it and around it; and from the appearance of his waist and downward I saw, as it were, the appearance of fire and brightness all around him.**

וָאֵרֶא כְּעֵין חַשְׁמַל כְּמַרְאֵה־אֵשׁ בֵּית־לָהּ סָבִיב מִמַּרְאֵה מָתְנָיו וּלְמָעְלָה וּמִמַּרְאֵה מָתְנָיו וּלְמַטָּה רָאִיתִי כְּמַרְאֵה־אֵשׁ וְנֹגַהּ לוֹ סָבִיב:

This Man has fire and electricity shooting around inside Him and coming out of Him. Verse 28 goes on to say there was an image of a rainbow surrounding him. This Man is the center and source of all the power. Here is the source of energy which, multiplied by the speed of light, brought physical matter into existence at the "big bang" of creation.

The vision of this Nuclear-power Man on the throne over the firmament gives insight as to what happened in Genesis chapter one. Put Ezekiel 1 together with Genesis 1, plus Quantum physics and Einstein's theory of relativity, and we have a clue as to how creation started.

With all the supernatural explosions and terrifying creatures, we could understand why some rabbis were hesitant to study the chapter. But the real problematic part is not the weird creatures and the nuclear cloud. The problem is that Man. He is what is so mind-blowing; and He is what the rabbis wanted to conceal.

An all-powerful God in the form of a man—that's THE revelation. The idea that God could be seen in the form of a man is what is so shocking. If God appeared in the form of a man to Abraham, Moses, Ezekiel and many of our prophets and patriarchs, then there is no contradiction between the faith of our forefathers and the divinity of the Messiah.

One may have a different view of who this God-Man was in Ezekiel chapter 1. However, the reality of His existence from a biblical point of view is undeniable. If almighty God appears in the form of a man, then there is no reason to reject outright the possibility that Yeshua could be divine. The concept of a God-Man is perfectly legitimate within the worldview of the Law and the Prophets.

Let's simplify the moral and logical challenge. The Law and the Prophets came before the New Covenant. If the New Covenant has a totally different concept of God, then the New Covenant is wrong, not the Law and the Prophets. The New Covenant presents Yeshua as the Son of God. The term "Son of God" means the revelation of God to mankind in the form of a man.

If the Law and the Prophets state that there can be no such thing as God appearing in a form like a human being, then the premise of the New Covenant is heretical at the very root. (And that is exactly why many sincere rabbis are so angry at Messianic Jews. They feel we are bringing a totally heretical view of God when we speak of the divinity of Yeshua.)

On the other hand, if the Law and the Prophets authorize and confirm that God can appear in the likeness of a man, then the revelation of Yeshua in the New Covenant is a plausible option. To our view, it is the obvious and necessary conclusion to the Hebrew Scriptures. In this study we have found repeatedly that a divine being in the form of a Man was the center of the faith of our forefathers. This revelation reasonably and logically leads to faith in Yeshua.

The Bible uses poetic and aesthetic language. I have been describing these divine appearances as a "God-Man-Angel." What could we call someone who is the image of the invisible God in human form? The simplest and most gracious way to say it is: Son.

In Second Temple Judaism, the idea that the Messiah would be called the Son of God was accepted (**Ps. 2:2, 7**). The disagreement in the gospels was not whether the Messiah could be called "the Son of God," but whether Yeshua was indeed that person (**Matt. 26:63; 27:40**).

The New Covenant calls Yeshua the Son of God. This is not referring to marital relations. It means that Yeshua is the God-Man-Angel who appeared to our forefathers. He is the human visible image of the invisible God. He is "Ben Elohim," the Son who has come forth from the Father and made Him manifest to mankind.

**John 1:18—No one has seen God at any time. The only begotten Son, who is in the bosom of the Father, He has made Him known.**

Whatever our limited brains can understand about God must be revealed to us in a form that a human can grasp. Whatever is knowable about God is found in Yeshua. He makes God knowable. We cannot see God. But we can know God through the Son of God. He is the manifestation of Him in human form (**Col. 1:15; 1 Tim. 3:16; Heb. 1:3**).

Ezekiel described the details of what and whom he saw in chapter one. However, that was not the only time he saw Him. The book of Ezekiel records that he saw the Lord in His glory five times! (In the other encounters he does not give the details of what he saw, since he already recorded that in Ezekiel 1.) Here is a brief citation of each:

**Ezekiel 1:26—On the likeness of the throne was a likeness with the appearance of a man.**

עַל דְּמוּת הַכִּסֵּא דְּמוּת כְּמַרְאֵה אָדָם

**Ezekiel 3:23**—The glory of Yehovah stood there, like the glory which I saw by the river Chebar; and I fell on my face.

כְּבוֹד־יְהֹוָה עֹמֵד כַּכָּבוֹד אֲשֶׁר רָאִיתִי עַל־נְהַר־כְּבָר
וָאֶפֹּל עַל־פָּנָי:

**Ezekiel 8:2-3**—Then I looked, and there was a likeness, like the appearance of fire - from the appearance of His waist and downward, fire; and from His waist upward, like the appearance of electric brilliance. He stretched out the form of a hand...

וָאֶרְאֶה וְהִנֵּה דְמוּת כְּמַרְאֵה־אֵשׁ מִמַּרְאֵה מָתְנָיו וּלְמַטָּה
אֵשׁ וּמִמָּתְנָיו וּלְמַעְלָה כְּמַרְאֵה־זֹהַר כְּעֵין הַחַשְׁמַלָה:
וַיִּשְׁלַח תַּבְנִית יָד...

**Ezekiel 10:1-2**—And I looked, and there in the firmament that was above the head of the cherubim, there appeared something like a sapphire stone, having the appearance of the likeness of a throne. Then He spoke...

וָאֶרְאֶה וְהִנֵּה אֶל־הָרָקִיעַ אֲשֶׁר עַל־רֹאשׁ הַכְּרֻבִים כְּאֶבֶן
סַפִּיר כְּמַרְאֵה דְּמוּת כִּסֵּא נִרְאָה עֲלֵיהֶם: וַיֹּאמֶר...

**Ezekiel 43:2, 3, 6-7**—And behold, the glory of the God of Israel came... like the vision which I saw by the river Chebar; and I fell on my face... Then I heard Him speaking to me... And He said to me, "Son of man, this is the place of My throne and the place of the soles of My feet..."

וְהִנֵּה כְּבוֹד אֱלֹהֵי יִשְׂרָאֵל בָּא... כְּמַרְאֵה הַמַּרְאֶה אֲשֶׁר
רָאִיתִי כַּמַּרְאֶה אֲשֶׁר־רָאִיתִי בְּבֹאִי לְשַׁחֵת אֶת־הָעִיר
וּמַרְאוֹת כַּמַּרְאֶה אֲשֶׁר רָאִיתִי אֶל־נְהַר־כְּבָר וָאֶפֹּל
אֶל־פָּנָי: וָאֶשְׁמַע מִדַּבֵּר אֵלָי... וַיֹּאמֶר אֵלַי בֶּן־אָדָם
אֶת־מְקוֹם כִּסְאִי וְאֶת־מְקוֹם כַּפּוֹת רַגְלָי...

On most of the occasions that Ezekiel saw these visions, he fainted. The Lord had to strengthen him. Had the Lord not protected him supernaturally, he might have died. In these visions notice the mention of the chair, the human-like body, the hand stretched out, and so on. These were repetitions of the same Glory and God-Man that Ezekiel saw in chapter one.

# CHAPTER ELEVEN
## *My Eyes Have Seen the King*

Isaiah also had an opportunity to see God in the form of a Man sitting on a chair, or throne. (He called Him "Adonai," the plural form of "Lord," which is normally used to refer to God.)

**Isaiah 6:1—In the year that King Uzziah died, I saw Adonai sitting on a throne, high and lifted up, and the train of His robe filled the temple.**

בִּשְׁנַת־מוֹת הַמֶּלֶךְ עֻזִּיָּהוּ וָאֶרְאֶה אֶת־אֲדֹנָי יֹשֵׁב
עַל־כִּסֵּא רָם וְנִשָּׂא וְשׁוּלָיו מְלֵאִים אֶת־הַהֵיכָל:

Isaiah also saw supernatural winged angelic creatures, here called Seraphim instead of Cherubim. They were crying out, "Holy, Holy, Holy…" This moment of holy adoration has become a model for worship in both the Jewish and Christian communities. In the Jewish world, it is called the *Kedushah*—קדושה.

Isaiah's response of repentance, faith and humility has touched all of our hearts. In contrast to the holiness of what he sees, Isaiah is aware of his own unworthiness.

**Isaiah 6:5—Woe unto me… for my eyes have seen the King, Yehovah of Armies.**

אוֹי־לִי ... כִּי אֶת־הַמֶּלֶךְ יְהוָה צְבָאוֹת רָאוּ עֵינָי:

It is reasonable to ask whether the God-Man that Isaiah saw was God the "Father" or God the "Son." To a certain extent either one of those answers would be acceptable. Our primary purpose is to show that throughout the Law and the Prophets, the God of Israel appears in a human-like form.

However, let us look at the question in more depth. In the New Covenant, John mentions Isaiah's vision several times. In his writings there is some reference which would indicate that Isaiah saw the Heavenly Father, but the majority of the references indicate that Isaiah saw Yeshua, the Messianic King.

**Revelation 4** reveals a moment of heavenly worship that is a composition of the elements both of Ezekiel chapter 1 and Isaiah chapter 6. John describes the four living creatures, a crystal firmament, and the flaming glory much as Ezekiel did (**Rev. 4:3-8**). He describes the "Holy, Holy, Holy" worship much as Isaiah did (**Rev. 4:8-9**). He describes the throne and the one who sat upon it, as both Ezekiel and Isaiah did (**Rev. 4:2-3**). Isaiah, Ezekiel and John all had glimpses of the same heavenly reality.

In Revelation 4, the one being worshiped is the Heavenly Father. This strongly suggests that Isaiah 6 and Ezekiel 1 were visions of the Heavenly Father as well. However, in the book of Revelation, Yeshua is also found sitting or standing upon the throne.

**Revelation 3:21—...as I also overcame and sat down with My Father on His throne.**

**Revelation 5:6—And I looked, and behold, in the midst of the throne and of the four living creatures, and in the midst of the elders, stood a Lamb as though it had been slain...**

**Revelation 7:17—For the Lamb who is in the midst of the throne...**

**Revelation 22:1—...proceeding from the throne of God and of the Lamb.**

**Revelation 22:3—The throne of God and of the Lamb shall be in it.**

In these passages, Yeshua is in the center or middle of the throne. (The word for "midst" in these verses is the Greek word *meso*, like mezzanine or Mesopotamia.) In royal throne rooms, there was enough sitting space for more than one person. [We see this for example when Bat Sheva sat together with Solomon on his throne (**1 Kings 2:19**, see also **Ps. 45:9**).] Therefore, from the references in the book of Revelation, the Isaiah 6 passage could be the Father or the Son.

[Note: Ezekiel and Isaiah saw a God-Man sitting on a throne. **First Kings 10:18-21** describes the construction of Solomon's throne.

It seems to be an earthly replica of the heavenly throne, just as the tabernacle was an earthly replica of the heavenly tabernacle (**Exod. 25:9, 40**). There is a heavenly throne and an earthly throne. God's will is for the one sitting on the heavenly throne to rule on the earthly throne as well.]

There is also a very important reference to Isaiah's vision in John 12:36-40 where John discusses a conflict between Yeshua and the local religious leaders. During that discussion, John quotes from Isaiah chapter 6. Then he makes this brief but pointed statement:

**John 12:41—These things Isaiah said when he saw His glory and spoke of Him.**

This verse is shocking. John states directly that Isaiah saw Yeshua glorified, not the Heavenly Father. Seeing Yeshua as the glorified king in Isaiah 6 changes our perspective greatly about Isaiah's vision of the kingdom of God on earth.

A third reason to see Isaiah's vision as describing Yeshua instead of the Father is the verse we quoted previously:

**John 1:18—No one has seen God at any time. The only begotten Son, who is in the bosom of the Father, He has declared Him.**

No one has seen God. Who was it that they did see? They saw Yeshua, the Son who makes God manifest to mankind. John's statement here is a general principle of interpreting the Law and the Prophets. Our forefathers did not see the Heavenly Father; the one they saw was Yeshua.

When Adam and Eve sinned in the Garden of Eden, the Bible says that they all of a sudden "saw" their nakedness. The fact that they saw their nakedness was not an **increase** of vision, but a **decrease** of vision. At that moment they saw carnal things, but lost sight of the spiritual things. This was not a small myopic loss of vision; this was an enormous fall into spiritual blindness. At that moment they stopped seeing an entire dimension of reality.

From the moment of the Fall, there was no practical purpose for human beings to see the Father. All judgment and relationship with human beings was delegated into the hands of Yeshua (**John 5:22**) until the plan of redemption would be completed. God is the

Father, but Yeshua is the savior. No man comes unto the Father except through Him (**John 14:6**). The only way to see God is through Yeshua alone (**John 14:9**).

There is another aspect to Isaiah's statement, **"Woe is me, for I am undone... for my eyes have seen the King" (Isa. 6:5).**

וַיֹּאמֶר אוֹי לִי כִי נִדְמֵיתִי... כִּי אֶת הַמֶּלֶךְ יְהוָה צְבָאוֹת רָאוּ עֵינָי.

The question has to do with the word "King." The role of the divine King ruling on this earth, and the picture of the kingdom of God on earth, is the central idea throughout the prophecies of the entire book of Isaiah. The revelation of the glorified King of Isaiah 6 is a turning point to understanding not only Isaiah, but the very concept of the kingdom of God.

Did Isaiah see a vision of God in heaven? Or did he see a glorified King who would one day rule upon the earth in David's stead? Ultimately the question involves whether there will be an earthly Messianic kingdom or whether eternal life consists only as spiritual beings in heaven. Will there be a literal Millennial kingdom or is it just figurative?

In Hebrew, nouns and verbs are similar to one another. A ruler is one who rules. A king is one who "kings," that is, who leads a government. Not only has Yeshua been assigned by God to be the savior of mankind, He has also been assigned to be the ruler of mankind.

The world-to-come will have a society of international peace and prosperity (**Isa. 2; Mic. 4**). There will be a government ruling that society; the Messiah will be the head of that government. Those who have walked in trustworthiness and righteousness in this life will rule and reign together with the Messiah in that future government (**Rev. 3:21; 5:10; 20:4; 20:6; Rom. 8:17; Matt. 19:28**).

In the modern State of Israel, there is a President and a Prime Minister. Legally the President is higher than the Prime Minister, but it is the Prime Minister who runs the country. The President receives all the diplomatic honors on behalf of the nation, but he is not allowed to be involved in the running of the government.

Our Heavenly Father is greater than Yeshua. Yeshua is submitted to Him. However, they have job descriptions which are different from one another; though they work together in unity. Yeshua is akin to the Prime Minister who runs the government of the kingdom of God. The kingdom belongs to the Father (**Matt. 6:10**), but as it comes to earth, it is Yeshua who is the king; He is the one who does the actual ruling. The Father is more like the President. It is not wrong to use the term "king" when referring to God the Father. However, the majority of the verses in the New Covenant that speak of "king" are not referring to the Father, but to Yeshua. This is significant.

Yeshua told a parable about a banquet in **Matthew 22** in which the Father is the king. Paul also refers to the Father as the king, living in eternal and invisible light (**1 Tim. 1:17; 6:15**). Yet, virtually all the other references to the divine king in the New Covenant are referring explicitly to Yeshua.

- Yeshua told Pilate He was born to be a king (**John 18:37**)

- Wise men from the East sought one born to be king of the Jews (**Matt. 2:2**)

- Yeshua is the descendant of King David (**Matt. 1:1**)

- Jerusalem is His capital, the city of the great King (**Matt. 5:35**)

- Yeshua is the King who came to Zion riding on a donkey (**Matt. 21:5**)

- Yeshua was crucified as King of the Jews (**Matt. 21:37**)

- Nethaniel recognized Him as the King of Israel (**John 1:49**)

- Yeshua was received with shouts of Hosanna, the King of Israel (**John 12:13**)

- Yeshua is the King of the saints (**Rev. 15:3**)

- He is the Lord of lords and King of kings (**Rev. 17:14; 19-16**)

What did Isaiah mean when he said he saw the king? Here the context is important. The passage is set in response to the death of Uzziah, king of Judah. In the wake of Uzziah's death, Isaiah has a vision in which he sees another king who will one day replace Uzziah. That king will be greater, more glorious. He is placed in juxtaposition to Uzziah.

Uzziah was one of David's direct descendants. Therefore, Yeshua is a descendant of Uzziah as well. Yeshua came to replace Uzziah for eternity. Yeshua's kingdom is the spiritual extension of David and Uzziah's kingdoms. The central theme of Isaiah's prophecies was the kingdom of God being established on earth, and the soon-coming king of that kingdom.

The vision of Yeshua lifted up in glory in Isaiah 6 is also set in contrast to the one who is being lifted up as the suffering servant in Isaiah 52-53.

**Isaiah 52:13—Behold My Servant will do wisely; he will be exalted and lifted up very high.**

$$\text{הִנֵּה יַשְׂכִּיל עַבְדִּי יָרוּם וְנִשָּׂא וְגָבַהּ מְאֹד:}$$

The Isaiah 6 exaltation must be understood in contrast to the King Messiah being lifted up in suffering in Isaiah 52-53. The One who is lifted up in suffering will be the same one lifted up in glory. The glorified one is the same as the suffering one (**Isa. 57:15**).

The king of glory in Isaiah 6 will bring the kingdom of God on earth. Yeshua is the king of glory. He suffered for our sins. He will save us and establish God's kingdom. He will reveal God's nature to us. He will rule and reign on this earth. That is the hope that accompanies the vision of the king from Isaiah 6.

Isaiah's vision of the exalted King in Isaiah 6 is part of the series of prophecies throughout the whole book of Isaiah that describes Yeshua and the coming of His Messianic kingdom. If we see Isaiah 6 as a vision of the Father, we miss the entire purpose and context of the book of Isaiah.

Isaiah starts with a vision in chapter 2 about the kingdom of God on earth. But in that vision, there is no king. Isaiah 2 is a kingdom without a king. Isaiah 6 is a king without a kingdom. The king of Isaiah 6 goes together with the kingdom in Isaiah 2.

Isaiah 7 and 9 speak of the birth of a supernatural baby boy who will be both king and divine. But in those prophecies, we do not see Him as an adult. Yeshua in Isaiah 6 is the grown up baby of promise from Isaiah 7 and 9. Isaiah 6 goes together with Isaiah 7 and 9.

Isaiah 40 (and many other chapters) speaks of the good news of a coming Messiah and His kingdom.

**Isaiah 40:9—Go up onto a high mountain, you who shares the good news with Zion. Lift up your voice with power, you who shares the good news with Jerusalem. Lift up your voice; do not be afraid; say to the cities of Judah, "Behold, here is your God."**

עַל הַר גָּבֹהַ עֲלִי לָךְ מְבַשֶּׂרֶת צִיּוֹן הָרִימִי בַכֹּחַ קוֹלֵךְ מְבַשֶּׂרֶת יְרוּשָׁלַ͏ִם הָרִימִי אַל־תִּירָאִי אִמְרִי לְעָרֵי יְהוּדָה הִנֵּה אֱלֹהֵיכֶם.

Isaiah 6 is the vision of the "king who is God" that Judah is being summoned to look at with their eyes. That is the king whom Isaiah saw. That is the divine king we are writing about here. Isaiah 6 goes together with Isaiah 40.

[Note: As I type these words, I am sitting on a hill in a suburb on the outskirts of Jerusalem. The name of this town is called "Who Shares the Good News with Zion." From here we are writing about Isaiah 6 and Isaiah 40, saying to Judah, "This glorified king is your God; it is Yeshua."]

Isaiah 52-53, as mentioned above, speaks of the suffering and crucifixion of the Messiah. The one glorified in Isaiah 6 is the one crucified in Isaiah 53. The one crucified in Isaiah 53 is the one glorified in Isaiah 6.

**"Ought not the Messiah to have suffered these things and to enter into His glory?"(Luke 24:26)** The Messiah must suffer

AND enter into His glory. Isaiah 53 must be seen together with Isaiah 6.

Isaiah 65-66 speaks of the renewal of Zion in the new creation. The renewal of Isaiah 65-66 takes place in the kingdom of Isaiah 2, led by the king of Isaiah 6, who was crucified in Isaiah 53. If we don't see the exalted one of Isaiah 6 as Yeshua, we miss the stream of thought in Isaiah's prophecies.

We could summarize the flow of Isaiah's kingdom prophecies this way:

**Isaiah 2:** the kingdom on earth with its capital in Jerusalem

**Isaiah 6:** the glorified Messianic king of that kingdom

**Isaiah 7, 9:** the divine child who would become the Messianic king

**Isaiah 35, 40:** proclaiming the good news of the coming kingdom

**Isaiah 42, 49:** good news proclaimed to nations of the world

**Isaiah 52-53:** Messianic king suffering to remove sin

**Isaiah 65-66:** renewal of creation in the new world of that kingdom

When our eyes see the king of Isaiah 6 as Yeshua, there is a consistent logic to the vision of the kingdom of God from the beginning of Isaiah unto the end.

Isaiah lived approximately 200 years after David. His prophecies deal with a theological problem. The kingdom of David and his sons was supposed to be the kingdom of God. However, the Davidic kingdom was plagued with political intrigue, sexual immorality and violent crime. This could not be the kingdom of God in and of itself. Isaiah began to envision an "improved" Davidic kingdom. He saw a new and better world coming. He saw the divine king who would rule in that kingdom.

Isaiah's prophecies (and all the Israelite prophets) form a bridge between the historical Davidic kingdom and the spiritual Messianic kingdom. Isaiah's prophecies are a middle stage: the first stage is David and Solomon's kingdoms; the second stage is the vision of the Israelite prophets; the third stage is the gospel of Yeshua and His disciples. The understanding of the kingdom of God developed through the years from David to Isaiah to Yeshua.

Metaphorically, we could see David's kingdom as the body; Isaiah's prophecies as the soul; and Yeshua's gospel as the spirit. If we do not see the bridge of Isaiah's prophecies, then the Davidic kingdom remains a political entity lacking the greater spiritual dimension, and the Church's vision of a heavenly kingdom remains a disembodied spiritual mysticism. The kingdom prophecies of Isaiah knit the two together in harmony.

The glorified king of Isaiah 6 is the key link between the two. When we see Isaiah 6 as the glorified Messianic king, then the heavenly aspects and the earthly aspects of the kingdom of God come together in perfect unity (**Zech. 14:9; Eph. 1:10**). The glorified king of Isaiah unites the heavenly kingdom and the earthly kingdom. He unites the Christian view and the Jewish view of the kingdom of God. That is the king that Isaiah's eyes saw. Our eyes will see Him one day as well.

[**Note:** Isaiah has sixty-six chapters. The Tanakh has thirty-nine books and the New Covenant has twenty-seven books. Thus the sixty-six chapters of Isaiah represent the sixty-six books of the Tanakh and New Covenant together. The fortieth chapter of Isaiah (equivalent to the first chapter of the New Covenant) represents a discernible change in style in Isaiah's writing, yet continues on the same theme. Isaiah 40 contains clear prophecies about the "preaching of the good news (gospel)—verses 3-11. Isaiah 40 is quoted in all the gospels as the basis of the teaching of John the Baptist in introducing Yeshua as the Messiah to the people of Israel.

The change in style is so dramatic that almost all non-religious universities teach that there were two different Isaiahs who wrote the book, one from chapter 1 to 39, and the other from 40 to 66. (Document criticism of Isaiah is much more complex than this, but almost all agree on multiple authors.) I believe there was one author because the theme of the kingdom of God is consistent from beginning to end. However, Isaiah's own thoughts developed through his life as he matured as a prophet.

In the same way, the New Covenant is a discernible leap forward in the revelation of the kingdom of God, yet it is a consistent development of the same vision that was proclaimed by the Hebrew prophets. Isaiah's prophecies are a development from David's kingdom; and the New Covenant is a development from Isaiah's prophecies. There is a consistent progressive revelation from the Davidic-Solomonic kingdom to the Israelite-Exilic prophets to the gospel message of Yeshua and His disciples.]

# CHAPTER TWELVE
## *The Son of Man*

Since God did appear throughout the Hebrew Bible in the form of a man, there is no reason to reject the premise of the New Covenant that Yeshua could be that "God-Man." Yeshua is the best candidate to fulfill that description. In fact, He is the only possible candidate who could fulfill that description. No one else in history has ever plausibly been suggested as such.

Yeshua is the open revelation of that "mystery man" from the Old Covenant. That is part of the "newness" of the New Covenant. What already existed in the Law and the Prophets in a veiled form has now become openly known to all.

The revelation of God to man in the form of a man is called the "Son" of God. The concept of the Messiah being called the "Son" of God was also introduced by the Israelite prophets before the New Covenant. (See for example **Ps. 2:7; 2 Sam. 7:14; Prov. 30:4; Isa. 7:14; Isa. 9:6; Dan. 3:25**.) If Yeshua is the Messiah, then He is that God-man, that "Son."

The revelation of God to man comes through the God-man. Our Heavenly Father has delegated that task to the Son. Almost without exception, the Heavenly Father is not seen. What people saw was the Son, Yeshua. This principle was summarized succinctly by John:

**John 1:18—No one has seen God at any time. The only begotten Son, who is in the bosom of the Father, He has declared Him.**

Yeshua is the manifestation of the Father (**John 14:6; 1 Tim. 3:16**). No one has ever seen the Father. The one who was seen by mankind was the Son. I know of only two exceptions to that rule: one in the Old Covenant (**Dan. 7**), and one in the New Covenant (**Rev. 5**).

In this chapter we want to ask the questions, "Why does the Father normally not appear? Why are the appearances of God made by the Son? Why does the Father appear together with Yeshua in these two exceptions?"

The revelation of God to mankind must come through someone who is a son of man himself. In biblical terms this is simply stated: "Because He is the Son of Man."

**Daniel 7:13-14**

**I was watching in the night visions, and behold, One like the Son of Man, coming with the clouds of heaven.**

**He came to the Ancient of Days, and they brought Him near before Him. Then to Him was given dominion and glory and a kingdom, that all the peoples, nations, and tongues should worship Him.**

**His dominion is an everlasting dominion, which shall not pass away; and His kingdom shall not be destroyed.**

חָזֵה הֲוֵית בְּחֶזְוֵי לֵילְיָא וַאֲרוּ עִם־עֲנָנֵי שְׁמַיָּא כְּבַר אֱנָשׁ

אָתֵה הֲוָה וְעַד־עַתִּיק יוֹמַיָּא מְטָה וּקְדָמוֹהִי הַקְרְבוּהִי:

וְלֵהּ יְהִיב שָׁלְטָן וִיקָר וּמַלְכוּ וְכֹל עַמְמַיָּא אֻמַיָּא

וְלִשָּׁנַיָּא לֵהּ יִפְלְחוּן שָׁלְטָנֵהּ שָׁלְטָן עָלַם דִּי־לָא יֶעְדֵּה

וּמַלְכוּתֵהּ דִּי־לָא תִתְחַבַּל:

This is one of the most explicit pictures of the Messiah in the Hebrew Bible. This prophecy sets the stage for the Messianic expectations that we find in the nation of Israel during the Second Temple period in the gospels.

The Ancient of Days is God our Heavenly Father. The Son of Man is the Messiah. The Messiah is brought before God. Great authority is delegated to Him. In fact, all authority is delegated to Him (**Matt. 28:18; Phil. 2:9**). All peoples worship and serve Him.

(**Note:** The word here in the Aramaic comes from the root פ-ל-ה, P-L-KH, which means both to worship in a religious adoration and also to serve as a common laborer. In Hebrew as well the root ע-ב-ד, U-B-D, means both work and worship. Work and worship are parallel thoughts. The point is that the word in Daniel for serve or worship implies both spiritual adoration and submission to authority.)

To our Jewish people, we say: This is our Messiah. He has all authority on earth. All the nations worship Him. He is brought before God on the clouds of heaven. Who else could this be if not Yeshua? Someone has to fulfill this prophecy. The Messiah must fit the description in this passage. If it were not Yeshua, it would have to be someone else exactly like Him. If the Messiah has not yet come, then he will be just like Yeshua when he does come.

One objection that Jewish people have to the messiah-ship of Yeshua is that many of our sages rejected Him and that many of the Gentiles accepted Him. Ironically, that is not proof against Yeshua's messiah-ship, but rather a proof for it. The Messiah had to be rejected in His own generation (**Ps. 118:22a; Isa. 53:3**), and be given authority over the Gentile nations (**Ps. 118:22b; Dan. 7:14**). We also see that pattern in Joseph (Yoseph) in the book of Genesis: he was rejected by his brothers, yet became a ruler in Egypt. For this reason, the Messiah is sometimes referred to as Ben Yoseph.

The Messiah is described above in **Daniel 7:13** as **"coming with the clouds of heaven."** That description is reminiscent of Elijah's ascent into heaven in a whirlwind (**2 Kings 2:11**). Yeshua ascended into heaven in a similar fashion (**Acts 1:10**). He will come back on those same clouds (**Acts 1:11**).

Why do the Ancient of Days and the Son of Man Messiah appear together in such a unique way in **Daniel 7**? One purpose is to demonstrate the transfer of authority. It would not be sufficient to show the Son alone or the Father alone. The authority must be delegated; the commission must be assigned; the anointing must be passed down. To show that delegation of authority, both of them must be seen together (just as David had to demonstrate the delegation of kingdom authority to Solomon—**1 Kings 1**).

The second place where the Father and the Son appear together is in **Revelation 5**. Here is a short excerpt:

**Revelation 5:6-7**

**And I looked, and behold, in the midst of the throne... stood a Lamb as though it had been slain... Then He came and took the scroll out of the right hand of Him who sat on the throne.**

The purpose in showing the Father and the Son together in this passage is slightly different from the one in Daniel 7. Yeshua is revealed in His full glory in **Revelation 1** (more on that in Section Five). After showing His full glory, the Scriptures must clarify at least one time the difference between Yeshua and the Father. If this clarification were not made, some might think that there is no Father, as if the Son were all; or that Yeshua is both the Father and the Son. That mistake was propagated by some as "Jesus only" theology. Seeing the two standing together in both **Daniel 7** and **Revelation 5** clarifies that misunderstanding.

God is manifested to mankind in the Son. The Father and the Son had to been seen together on two occasions, one in the Prophets and one in the New Covenant. There were two purposes: the first to show delegation of authority; the second to clarify the distinction between the Father and the Son. Reading the passages in Daniel 7 and Revelation 5 together leave no doubt as to their separate roles.

The writings of John have a special dimension of spiritual revelation. The gospel of John was written later than the first three. The first three gospels concentrate on telling *what* happened in Yeshua's ministry; John's concentrates on *why* it happened. John chapter 14 deals with the issue of why Yeshua is given the role of bringing the revelation of God to mankind instead of the Father.

Yeshua's disciples realize that He is the Messiah. They ask Him to show them the Father's glory (similar to Moses' request in **Exodus 33**). Yeshua replies that it is not necessary for them to see the Father. What they see in Him is enough to know what the Father is like. All the revelation that the Father would want to give to them is already found in Yeshua.

**John 14:9-10—He who has seen Me has seen the Father; so how can you say, "Show us the Father?" Do you not believe that I am in the Father, and the Father is in Me?**

All the revelation of God to man is inside the God-Man. The reason for this is that God has a plan for mankind. Part of God's destiny for man is to impart into us divine attributes (**2 Pet. 1:3-4**). Imparting divine attributes to man is most effectively done through a man who has those divine attributes Himself. God's purpose for the human race was planned out before the foundation of the world (**Eph. 1:4-11**). His plan is for our benefit. [For a list of verses on God's predestined plan, see appendix #9 on "Before the Foundation."]

Because the plan includes men, it cannot proceed any faster than men will be able to receive it. The revelation of God *to* men is the revelation of God *for* men, and therefore must come *through* a man. The reason that the plan comes through Yeshua is that He is the Son of Man. The plan for humans is through a human. If God's plan were only for angels, then being the Son of God would be sufficient. But since God's plan is for mankind, that plan must be expressed through someone who is a man, the Son of Man.

God the Father cannot give up His glory, come off the throne, and take on the role of a servant to mankind. That is the task of the Son (**Phil. 2:6-8**). He is the bridge between God and mankind. He came from God to man as a man for the benefit of man. He will restore mankind into God's destiny for them.

For this reason, Yeshua uses the word "greater" twice in John 14. He says that the Father is greater than He (**John 14:28**). He also says that the disciples will do greater works than He (**John 14:12**). In these statements Yeshua expresses not only love and humility, but also the focus of His mission. He has come from the Father (who is greater) to lift up mankind (to do greater). Yeshua's mission was delegated to Him by the Father in order to bring mankind into our destiny.

Yeshua didn't come to seek His own greatness. He came to show us the Father's greatness, and to bring us into the greatness the Father has planned for us. (Of course His willingness to sacrifice Himself for others is what makes Yeshua so great Himself.) Yeshua came as God in the image of man to help us become man in the image of God (**Gen. 1:26**).

In order to accomplish the pre-destined plan of God, there must be someone who is both the image of God to man, and man in the image of God. This requires someone to be both God and Man. That's the genius of God's plan which comes through Yeshua. There is no reason for God to reveal Himself to mankind at this stage. What is for man must happen through a Man. The Father is greater than Yeshua. However, the fullness of God's plan is contained in Yeshua because He is God and man in one.

The first visitation of the God-Man to mankind is recorded in **Genesis 3:8** where Adam and Eve **"heard the sound of Yehovah God walking in the garden."** Had this been a few hours earlier, before their fall into sin, this might have been God the Father. However, since they had already fallen, we can assume this was Yeshua. At that moment, He began His mission of redemption.

There are many reasons why all authority has been given to Yeshua from the Father. Yeshua has authority to save man (**John 3:16**), judge man (**John 5:27**) and govern man (**Dan. 7:13**). He can be our intermediary (**1 Tim. 2:5**), our attorney (**1 John 2:1**) and our high priest (**Heb. 4:15**). Yeshua can fulfill all these functions because He is human as well as divine. He has all authority *because He is the Son of Man.*

**John 5:27—The Father has given Him authority to execute judgment, because He is the Son of Man.**

Let's summarize a few of the reasons why God's revelation to mankind comes through the Son and not the Father:

1. **Peer:** For justice to be done to men, they must be held accountable by a just standard. That judgment must come from one who is a "peer," who can understand what humans experience.

2. **Indwelling:** God created us because He desired to dwell inside us. Therefore God's plan focuses on a Man who is totally filled with His Spirit. Yeshua is that man where the fullness of God dwelled in bodily form (**Col. 2:9**).

3. **Potential:** God desires to bring us into a divine destiny as partakers of His nature (**2 Pet. 1:4**). Therefore the

model of this plan must be a human with totally divine attributes.

4.  **Atonement:** For forgiveness of sins we need an atoning sacrifice as a substitution. It must be life for life, soul for soul (**Lev. 17:11**). An animal is not enough; God the Father is too much. Only Yeshua fits the need.

5.  **Protection:** Since human beings have all sinned, direct exposure to God's glory power would kill us. God separates us from Himself for our own safety and sends Yeshua in His stead to redeem us.

6.  **Relationship:** We were created not just to be servants but to be friends (**John 15:15**). The only way to build fellowship with men is through a Man. Yeshua is the beginning of friendship between God and man.

7.  **Punishment:** Part of the reason we can't see the Father today is the result of our sin. Separation is our punishment (**Isa. 59:2**); seeing Him again will be our privilege at the end if we are faithful.

8.  **Government:** If there is to be a real kingdom of God on earth, it must include real people. There will be a society of people living together. That will require a godly government to organize the people. Yeshua came as a human and divine king to establish righteous government among the people of God.

9.  **Planet Earth:** God created the universe with heaven and earth (**Gen. 1:1**). He wants both elements in harmony. Today there is a breach between the two. Only someone who is a member of both can unify them. The fullness of God's plan is to bring heaven and earth together in Yeshua (**Eph. 1:10**).

10. **Understanding:** Like the parable of the elephant becoming an ant to explain to the ant about the nature of an elephant; so must God come in the form of a man for man to understand who God is.

11. **Pleasure:** God designed His plan around a "Son" because He wanted to. It is His own good pleasure (**Eph. 1:5**). As any dad, coach or pastor knows, there is more pleasure in having a child or disciple do something instead of yourself. God enjoys seeing His "sons" succeed.

12. **Intermediary:** When God's glory came on Mount Sinai, the people ran away. God had to send Moses to go back and forth from the mountain, because the people were afraid to come close to God (**Deut. 5:5**). Similarly, God sent Yeshua as the intermediary between mankind and God until all is reconciled (**1 Tim. 2:5; Deut. 18:15**).

The word for "man" in Hebrew is the same as the name "Adam." So when the Bible speaks of the Son of Man, it could also be written as the "Son of Adam." God created Adam in Genesis and gave him authority over this planet (**Gen. 1:26; Ps. 115:16**). Yeshua had to come as a son of Adam in order to take back the authority that Adam lost.

Why is the revelation of God to mankind primarily through a God-Man? Because God loves mankind and has a plan for us. He sent Yeshua to save us from sin and to bring us into that divine destiny (**John 3:16**). Yeshua could do this because He is not only the Son of God, but also because He is the Son of Man (**John 5:27**).

# PART FIVE

# The Revelation

---

In this section, we examine the appearances of the Divine Messenger as a glorified Man of fire to the prophet Daniel in Babylon and to the apostle John on Patmos.

We discover how the connection between these two ultimate appearances of the glorified Man of fire reveals the full divinity and identity of the Messiah. We will discuss how the Revelation of John is the final revelation of God to mankind.

Finally, we will summarize our study about God revealing Himself to mankind through a Man.

# Chapter Thirteen

# Who is the Man on Fire?

The God-Man-Angel appeared to prophets and patriarchs in so many forms and on so many occasions that the subject seems never-ending. That is exactly the impression the early disciples had.

**Luke 24:25, 27—...in all that the prophets spoke... And beginning at Moses and all the Prophets, and explained to them in all Scriptures the things concerning Himself.**

This was Yeshua's methodology on how to share the good news of the Messiah.

**Luke 24:44-45—"All things must be fulfilled which were written in the Torah of Moses, and in the Prophets and in the Psalms concerning Me." And He opened their hearts to understand the Scriptures.**

There are so many references to Yeshua in the Tanakh (Law, Prophets and Writings), that it is virtually impossible to exhaust the topic. [Notice Yeshua uses the traditional Jewish terminology of dividing the Hebrew Scriptures into three sections.]

**Acts 10:43—Of Him all the prophets bore witness...**

It seems like all the prophets wrote about Him.

**Acts 24:14—I serve the God of my forefathers, believing all things which are written in the Law and in the Prophets.**

The apostles' approach to Scriptures should be our approach. The study of the Messianic kingdom in the Law and the Prophets has been somewhat lost to both the Jewish and Christian worlds. Yet this use of the Tanakh was foundational to the worldview of the apostles. I believe this "full counsel" (**Acts 20:27**) scriptural approach to the kingdom of God will be restored in our generation.

**Acts 26:22—Saying no other things than those which the Prophets and Moses said would come...**

When the disciples heard Yeshua teaching the passages about Himself in the Law and the Prophets, their hearts burned (**Luke 24:32**). My heart still burns as I see all these passages about the Messiah and the Angel-Yehovah in the Tanakh. I hope yours does too.

**Acts 28:23—He bore witness from the morning to the evening and explained to them about the kingdom of God, persuading them about Yeshua from the Torah of Moses and from the Prophets.**

There are many places that Yeshua appears which may not seem obvious at first glance. Let's look at a few examples:

**Moses:** It was Yeshua who stood on the rock that brought forth water to Moses and the children of Israel (**Exod. 17:6**). [There is a veiled reference to this passage in **1 Cor. 10:4**. The rock was not just a symbol of Yeshua; He was standing there. How else would Moses have known to write that?]

**Samuel:** Yeshua stands next to Samuel's bed and calls to him (**1 Sam. 3:10**). Here, as in other places, He is referred to as Word-Yehovah. This is one of the meanings of the phrase in **John 1:1 and 14** that Yeshua was the Word of God which became flesh.

**Solomon:** Yeshua appeared twice to King Solomon, before Solomon fell into sin. He provided Solomon with the spirit of wisdom and revelation (**1 Kings 3:5; 9:2**). Saul (Paul) prayed that we also could receive that wisdom through Yeshua (**Eph. 1:17-21**); this was a New Covenant extension of Solomon's prayer.

**Elijah:** The Angel-Yehovah, spoke to Elijah three times (**1 Kings 19:7; 2 Kings 1:3; 1:15**). He sent Elijah on his mission, gave him prophetic words, and accompanied him in danger.

**Amos:** Amos the prophet saw the God-Man twice: once in a human form standing next to a wall with a plumb line in His hand (**Amos 7:7**); and another time standing next to the altar (**Amos 9:1**).

[For a more complete reference list of the appearances God in the form of a man in the Hebrew Scriptures, see Appendix #1 on "Divine Appearances in the Hebrew Bible."]

There is another lesser known appearance of Yeshua in the prophets, which has tremendous significance. This will be our last study reference.

**Daniel 10:5-6**

**I lifted my eyes and looked, and behold, a certain man clothed in linen, whose waist was girded with the gold of Uphaz.**

**His body was like a Tarshish jewel, his face like the appearance of lightning, his eyes like torches of fire, his arms and feet like burnished bronze; and the sound of his words was like the voice of a multitude.**

וָאֶשָּׂא אֶת־עֵינַי וָאֵרֶא וְהִנֵּה אִישׁ־אֶחָד לָבוּשׁ בַּדִּים
וּמָתְנָיו חֲגֻרִים בְּכֶתֶם אוּפָז: וּגְוִיָּתוֹ כְתַרְשִׁישׁ וּפָנָיו
כְּמַרְאֵה בָרָק וְעֵינָיו כְּלַפִּידֵי אֵשׁ וּזְרֹעֹתָיו וּמַרְגְּלֹתָיו
כְּעֵין נְחֹשֶׁת קָלָל וְקוֹל דְּבָרָיו כְּקוֹל הָמוֹן:

What makes this seemingly obscure reference explode with meaning is the fact that this description is quoted almost word for word by John in Revelation as describing Yeshua. The description is so similar that we have no choice but to understand that it is referring to the same person.

**Revelation 1:12-16**

**Then I turned to see the One speaking with me...**

**...one like the Son of Man, clothed with a garment down to His feet and girded around His chest with a golden band.**

**His head and hair were white like wool, as white as snow: and His eyes were like a flame of fire; His feet were like burnished brass, as if refined in a furnace; and His voice was like the sound of many waters.**

**...And His face was like the sun shining in its strength.**

Was John simply quoting Daniel? Or do the passages sound identical because what they saw was exactly the same? Let's understand this in both directions. 1) The glorified Man in the book of Daniel is no ordinary angel; it is Yeshua. 2) The Yeshua of the book of Revelation appears in Daniel and his prophecies.

The last three chapters of Daniel are a summary of what this Man said to him. Those prophecies are a precursor to the prophecies in the book of Revelation. Both Daniel and John had the same source.

A major section of Daniel's book was a prophecy about the future that he received from Yeshua. Daniel had a revelation from Yeshua just as John had a revelation from Him. Their experiences were quite similar.

There is also a connection with the mystery man of the fiery furnace. When Daniel's three friends, Hananiah, Azariah and Mishael, refused to obey Nebuchadnezzar's demand to worship his idol, they were thrown in a furnace. Immediately Nebuchadnezzar is shocked to notice there is a fourth person on the inside. And guess who it is? Yes, the Son of God.

**Daniel 3:25—And the king answered and said: behold I see four men walking around in the midst of the fire and there is no injury to them; and the appearance of the fourth is like the son of God**.

עָנֵה וְאָמַר הָא־אֲנָה חָזֵה גֻּבְרִין אַרְבְּעָה שְׁרַיִן מַהְלְכִין בְּגוֹא־נוּרָא וַחֲבָל לָא־אִיתַי בְּהוֹן וְרֵוֵה דִּי רביעיא דָּמֵה לְבַר־אֱלָהִין:

This wasn't just any son of God, but the Son of God. This is another example that the term "Son of God" was a known term throughout the ancient Middle East and not just a fabrication of the gospel writers.

The Son of God in Daniel 3 is the same as the Man of Fire in Daniel 10. One who has fire emanating out of his whole body from head to toe wouldn't have any difficulty walking around in a fire from a furnace. (Likewise when we have the fire of God in our hearts, nothing on the outside can hurt us.)

The more important aspect of the connection between Daniel 10 and Revelation 1 is what it means for our understanding of Yeshua and of the Angel-Yehovah. The book of Revelation is the culminating revelation of who Yeshua is.

The book of Revelation starts with the description of Yeshua in His glorified form. It is saying: You have not understood all the aspects of who Yeshua is by reading the gospels. In the gospels He does not appear in a glorified form (except for a brief moment on the Mount of Transfiguration—**Matt. 17; Luke 9**). There is another dimension of Yeshua that has not yet been revealed to you.

Yeshua in the New Covenant and Angel-Yehovah of the Tanakh appear at times in a glorified form and at times in a non-glorified form. [For a further discussion on the difference between these two forms, see Appendix #10, "Human and Glorified Appearances."]

The end-time prophecies in the book of Revelation start on this one point: Yeshua is revealed to be the Angel-Yehovah from the Old Covenant. We see the Angel-Yehovah in the Prophets. We see Yeshua in the gospels. The last book of the Bible puts the two together. The book of Revelation is the link between the Yeshua of Galilee and the Angel of Yehovah.

The main purpose of Revelation chapter 1 is to confirm this link between Yeshua and the Angel-Yehovah. It verifies the understanding that Yeshua and Angel-Yehovah are one and the same. The book of Revelation is not just about the End Times. It is the final revelation of who Yeshua is. This is also our goal in the last section of this book. We want to see Yeshua as John saw Him. We want to understand Yeshua as John understood Him.

Through the book of Revelation, God wants to give us the final realization that Yeshua is the same central Persona that appears throughout the Bible. He was the same glorified Man in Daniel, Ezekiel, and every other place in the Torah and the Prophets.

**Hebrews 13:8—Yeshua the Messiah is the same yesterday, today and forever.**

Yeshua is the same in eternity past and eternity present. Therefore we can see Him in all His appearances, not just in the gospels, but from Genesis to Revelation, from beginning to end.

**Revelation 1:8, 17—I am the Alpha and the Omega, the beginning and the end...**

**I am the first and the last.**

In Hebrew, the word "beginning" and the name "Genesis" is the same—*Bereshit*—בראשית. Yeshua is the same from Genesis to Revelation.

A central thesis of the book of Revelation is that Yeshua is the Angel-Yehovah. Thus the book of Revelation brings into harmony the appearances of the God-Man in the Old Covenant with the person of Yeshua in the New Covenant.

Revelation chapter 1 presents us with a dual challenge. 1) If we want to understand who Yeshua is in His glorified form, study all His appearances as Angel-Yehovah in the Law and the Prophets. 2) If we want to understand the Law and the Prophets, realize that the Angel-Yehovah is Yeshua in His pre-birth form. That is the dual revelation that we have been studying together throughout this book.

# CHAPTER FOURTEEN
## *John's Divine Revelation*

There was a development in the understanding of ancient Israel about the nature of God, the identity of the Angel of Yehovah, and the coming of the Messianic King. It was not in the realm of possibility at that time to put all the "pieces of the puzzle" together. By the time we reach the Second Temple period at the start of the gospels, there is a fervent expectation of the coming of the Messiah.

In the New Covenant, there is also a development in the understanding of the divinity of Yeshua in the minds of His disciples. We see Peter first get the revelation that Yeshua is the Messiah (**Matt. 16:16**). Peter's revelation established the first level, the rock, upon which the Church and the further understanding of Yeshua's identity would be built.

Paul then received another major level of heavenly revelation that boosted the Church into a greater dimension. He saw Yeshua as the divine Christ, head of the international Church (**Eph. 1:20-22; 2 Cor. 12:2-4; Gal. 1:12; 2:2, 6**). Even Peter admitted that Paul grasped things that he still didn't understand (**2 Pet. 3:16**).

Later, both in the book of Revelation and in his gospel, John rises to another level. John's revelation was the final stage in the scriptural development. Peter had the revelation to preach the gospel to the people of Israel. Paul had the revelation to establish the international Church. John had the revelation to prepare Israel and the Church for the Second Coming of Yeshua.

Peter's revelation was national and Israeli; Paul's was universal and international; John's was heavenly and eternal. In the synoptic gospels and Acts, Yeshua is the Messiah, king of Israel. In the epistles, Yeshua is the Christ, head of the Church. In John's gospel and Revelation, Yeshua is Yehovah, the manifestation of God. [For more on this topic, see Appendix # 11, "Divine and Davidic."]

Here are seven examples from John's teachings that identify Yeshua with the Yehovah of the Law and the Prophets:

## 1. I Am

Throughout the gospel of John, Yeshua says of Himself, "I am." There are over a dozen prophetic declarations of Yeshua's "I am." The first reference is Yeshua saying "I am He" to the Samaritan woman at the well (**John 4:26**); the last reference is Yeshua saying "I am He," and knocking down the soldiers that came to arrest Him (**John 18:5**). These references were John's way of identifying Yeshua with the "I AM THAT I AM" of **Exodus 3:14.** John believed that it was Yeshua who appeared to Moses in the bush; and that the name Yehovah refers to Him.

This was also John's way of identifying Yeshua with the many "I am" statements of Isaiah chapters 41 through 49. **"Come near to Me and hear this: I have not spoken in secret from the beginning; From the time of being, I was there.**

**And now Adonai Yehovah and His Spirit have sent Me." (Isa. 48:16)**

קִרְבוּ אֵלַי שִׁמְעוּ זֹאת לֹא מֵרֹאשׁ בַּסֵּתֶר דִּבַּרְתִּי מֵעֵת
הֱיוֹתָהּ שָׁם אָנִי· וְעַתָּה אֲדֹנָי יְהוִה שְׁלָחַנִי וְרוּחוֹ.

Here again we have a figure claiming divinity who was sent from God. He was both God and sent from God.

## 2. The Word

Yeshua is referred to as the Word of God. That is a reference to God creating the world by His words, "Let there be…"

## John 1:1—In the beginning was the Word, and the Word was with God, and the Word was God.

This expression is also referring to the appearances of the Word of God as the divine messenger who came to visit the prophets. The "Word" is both the message and the messenger. The prophets sometimes saw and heard, sometimes felt the presence and heard, and other times just heard.

Yeshua being the Word means that He came and spoke to someone personally. Two clear examples are: 1) where Abraham both saw and heard the word (**Gen. 15:1**), and 2) where the word comes and stands next to Samuel (**1 Sam. 3:7, 10**).

**Genesis 15:1—And after these things the Word-Yehovah came to Abram in a vision…**

אַחַר הַדְּבָרִים הָאֵלֶּה הָיָה דְבַר־יְהוָה אֶל־אַבְרָם בַּמַּחֲזֶה לֵאמֹר ...

**1 Sam. 3:7, 10—Now Samuel did not yet know Yehovah, nor was Word-Yehovah yet revealed to him.**

**And Yehovah came and stood and called out as at the other times, "Samuel, Samuel!"**

וּשְׁמוּאֵל טֶרֶם יָדַע אֶת־יְהוָה וְטֶרֶם יִגָּלֶה אֵלָיו דְּבַר־יְהוָה:

וַיָּבֹא יְהוָה וַיִּתְיַצַּב וַיִּקְרָא כְפַעַם־בְּפַעַם שְׁמוּאֵל שְׁמוּאֵל וַיֹּאמֶר שְׁמוּאֵל

It is interesting to note in both these verses the "Word of Yehovah" is in paired-noun construct in the Hebrew. "Word" and "Yehovah" are hyphenated together. The Scriptures do not say, "Word of the Lord" but "Word-Yehovah." The Genesis and Samuel passages are astonishing and only make sense in the light of John's understanding of Yeshua as the Word of Yehovah.

Word-Yehovah comes and visits Abraham and Samuel. To know Yehovah is to know this "Word-Yehovah." John understood Yeshua to be that prophetic Word who came to visit our forefathers.

### 3. The Author of the Ten Commandments

We discussed in Section Two the passage in **John 8:6** about Yeshua writing with His finger on the ground in response to the religious challenge concerning the death penalty for adultery. That reference identified Him with the Angel-Yehovah who wrote the Ten Commandments with the "finger of God" according to

**Exodus 31:18.** John understood Yeshua to be the one who wrote the Ten Commandments.

### 4. Abraham's Visitor

We discussed in Section One the passage about Yeshua having seen and known Abraham and having existed before Abraham (**John 8:56**). That reference identified Him with the Yehovah visitor who came with two angels to eat lunch with Abraham (**Gen. 18:1**). John understood Yeshua to be Abraham's visitor.

### 5. Joshua's Commander

We discussed in Section Three the connection between the **Joshua 5:13** Commander who came to fight at Jericho and the **Revelation 19:11** Commander who fights at the Second Coming. John believed the Commander who appeared to Joshua to be Yeshua.

### 6. Isaiah's King

We discussed in Section Four that **John 12:41** directly identifies the glorified King of **Isaiah 6:1** to be Yeshua. John believed that Isaiah's King was Yeshua, which is also substantiated by the context of kingdom prophecies throughout the book of Isaiah.

### 7. The Glorified Man in Ezekiel's and Daniel's Visions

We discussed in section four that John had virtually the same vision in **Revelation 4** that Ezekiel had in **Ezekiel 1.** John believed that the glorified Man over the Cherubim was Yeshua (**Rev. 3:21; 5:6; 7:17**). This was confirmed by John's associating the man of fire in **Daniel 10:5** with his vision of the glorified Yeshua in **Revelation 1:12.**

These examples give a brief outline of John's overall view that Yeshua was the eternal God-Man who made God manifest to mankind from the beginning of time. John also believed that Yeshua existed before the foundations of the world.

**John 17:5—...Glorify Me together with Yourself, with the glory which I had with You before the foundation of the world.**

**John 17:24—...Because You loved Me before the foundation of the world.**

If Yeshua existed before creation, it would certainly be logical that He would have been available and active during all the years of Israelite history leading up to the gospels. If so, where was He? And what was He doing? The answer should be self-evident by now.

The viewpoint shared in this book about Yeshua's identity is not found primarily in the gospels, Acts or the epistles. This revelation is part of the world view of John's writings, which was the last stage of development in the apostles' understanding of Yeshua's divinity.

[It is interesting how God uses the opposite of human talents to accomplish His purposes. Peter was an uneducated secular fisherman from the Galilee, and God used him to preach to the intensely educated religious leaders in Jerusalem. Paul was a self-righteous ultra-Orthodox Yeshiva student in Jerusalem, and God sent him out to establish the international Church among the Gentiles. John was Yeshua's most intimate friend on the human side. He was the one whom God used to reveal Yeshua's most fiery and heavenly side.]

John knew Him as both man and God. We likewise believe that Yeshua is both man and God.

**Romans 1:3-4**

**...Concerning His Son Yeshua the Messiah our Lord, who was born of the seed of David according to the flesh, and according to the Holy Spirit was demonstrated to be the Son of God in power by the resurrection from the dead...**

Once I was meditating on this passage. Yeshua is described as the seed of David (v. 3) and Son of God (v. 4). I sensed in my heart the question as to which of the two was more important. I thought, "Of course, being the Son of God is more important." Then I perceived the leading of the Holy Spirit saying, "No." I was surprised and asked within my heart, "Is being the son of David more important?!" Then I sensed the Holy Spirit witness again saying, "No." I was perplexed. Finally the solution came in the still voice within: "That He is both together." The key to understanding the Messiah is that He is both divine and human.

In recent years, among the Israeli Messianic leadership, both sides of the issue were debated. There is a small group of leaders who deny Yeshua's divinity; there is another small group who deny his humanity. However, the vast majority of the pastors and elders stand firmly with His dual nature.

How we see Yeshua affects how we see ourselves. We are made in the image of God (**Gen. 1:27**). Yeshua is that image of God for us and in us. Those who see themselves as descended from apes will necessarily have a low opinion of human nature. Our origins determine our outcome. We see ourselves not as evolving from apes, but as repenting of our sins and becoming glorified sons of God in the image of Yeshua.

How we see Him is how we see our destiny. With each stage of revelation of who Yeshua is, there is a corresponding development in the revelation of our own destiny in Him. We are in Him and He is in us. Each level of identity has a corresponding new level of authority.

The revelation of Yeshua as king of Israel was given to Simeon (Peter) in **Matthew 16**. Yeshua told Simeon that this revelation was not human or natural, but heavenly and supernatural (**v. 17**). At that moment, Peter received spiritual authority such that whatever he would bind or loose on earth would be done so in heaven (**vv. 18-19**). The same is true for anyone today who comes to faith in the same revelation that Simeon Peter had.

The revelation of Yeshua as head of the Church was given to Saul (Paul) in **Ephesians 1.** Yeshua has ascended into heaven over all powers and principalities (**vv. 20-21**). This understanding was given to Saul by revelation. He prayed for us to have the same enlightenment (**vv. 17-18**). That enlightenment will impart to us the same power and authority that Yeshua has, both in this world and the world to come. We are seated with Him spiritually in heaven (**Eph. 2:6-7**).

The first stage of our destiny is revealed to us through Peter in the gospels; the second stage through Paul in the epistles. The ultimate stage is through John in the book of Revelation.

As we meditate on the vision of Yeshua in the book of Revelation, a change takes place in us. As we grasp who He really is, so do we grasp who we really are in Him. His eyes are a flame of fire. He wears many crowns. He is dressed in white, with a gold band on His chest and a sword coming out of His mouth. His hair is like wool and His face is shining like the sun.

When that picture gets IN us, it makes us different. Fire comes out of our eyes. There is new power, passion and purity. Holiness and zeal burns out carnality and worldliness. We see a heavenly perspective of the kingdom. We are made ready for His coming, and made ready for the spiritual warfare leading up to that coming. Grace is imparted to our souls.

May God grant us the understanding of who Yeshua is as was revealed to Peter, Paul and John! And may we be changed to be like Him.

# SUMMARY

# *The Mystery Man*

---

*This additional section is designed to serve two purposes. First, it is a short summary of what we have learned in this book. It cites the most important references in a concentrated and abbreviated form.*

*Second, it is written in a format appropriate to be given to someone who is not yet a believer in Yeshua, whether of secular academic background or of Jewish religious background. Feel free to copy it and use it separately as a tool for creating dialogue and discussion.*

## The Mystery Man

There is an astonishing figure who appears throughout the Hebrew Bible. He is at one and the same time a messenger from God and yet divine himself. Is he a man, an angel, or God? He appears many times to our forefathers. Let's look at a few key examples. (It would be worth following along in the Bible to be able to verify the texts for yourself.)

## To Abraham

Most of us have grown up with the impression that it is impossible to see God and that He has no visible form. And certainly that God would not appear in the form of a man. Yet with Abraham our father, that is exactly what happened.

It is recorded that while Abraham was at the oaks of Mamre, God came to visit him in person in the form of a man.

### Genesis 18:1-2

**Then the Lord appeared to him by the oaks of Mamre, as he was sitting in the tent door in the heat of the day. So he lifted his eyes and looked, and behold, three men were standing by him; and when he saw them, he ran from the tent door to meet them, and bowed himself to the ground.**

Abraham saw three men. Two of the three were the angels who went on to Sodom to destroy the city (**Gen. 19:1**). The third of the three men is referred to throughout the chapter as YHVH, and Abraham relates to him as God in every way.

At the same time this person acts like a man in every sense, even eating a meal that included meat and milk. Abraham and this "man" discuss Sarah's upcoming birth of Isaac, as well as the impending destruction of Sodom. This "man" even takes credit for causing Sarah to have a baby after her long period of barrenness. Abraham talks to him as if he had the authority to decide whether to destroy Sodom or not. And this "man" is assumed to have the "fire power" to execute that decision.

Who could this person be? He couldn't be God because he appears as a man and acts like a man. On the other hand he couldn't be a man because Abraham refers to him as God in all authority and divinity. The person seems to have all of the attributes of both God and man. He seems to be a God-Man, or God in the form of a man, who came to earth to visit Abraham.

## To Jacob

This God or man makes another appearance to Jacob as well. Jacob is returning to the land of Israel after a long exile, having worked for his father-in-law Laban. He is fearful about meeting his brother Esau, who the last time he saw him (twenty years ago), had threatened to kill him. At night, as he prepares to cross the Jabok river, Jacob has an unusual experience with a mysterious man.

**Genesis 32:24**

**Then Jacob was left alone; and a man wrestled with him until the break of dawn.**

During this wrestling match, the man gave Jacob a pulled muscle in the back of the thigh. Jacob asks the man to bless him; in response the man changes Jacob's name to Israel. When the man leaves, Jacob calls the place Peniel (the face of God), because he believes that the man he wrestled with was actually God.

**Genesis 32:30**

**I have seen God face to face, and my life is preserved.**

In case Jacob might have thought this whole encounter was just his imagination, he notices that for the next few weeks he is walking with a limp from the pain in his thigh. This was a real physical encounter with someone that Jacob claimed to be God.

In case there was any doubt, the Torah confirms again that the person who blessed Jacob at Peniel was indeed "Elohim," God Himself, and even confirms the covenant promises He made to Abraham (**Gen. 35:9-13**).

This person is called God by Jacob and by the Torah. Yet he is also called a "man." He physically wrestles with Jacob all night, but also assumes the authority of God in the Abrahamic covenant. How could this be? Who could this be? Is he God or is he a man?

## To Moses

Moses also has a number of encounters with a mysterious being. This time the person is at times an angel and at times YHVH himself. The first time he meets him is at the burning bush. In Exodus 3:2, this person is called the angel of the Lord, but immediately after that, in verse 4, this same person is called God and YHVH.

**Exodus 3:2—And the angel of YHVH appeared to him in a flame of fire from the midst of a bush.**

**Exodus 3:4—So when YHVH saw that he turned aside to look, God called to him from the midst of the bush.**

Notice the phrase "in the midst of the bush." In verse 2 it is the angel in the midst of the bush. In verse 4 it is God in the midst of the bush. They were both in the bush. What happened? Were there two people who switched places? Was there just the angel who spoke on behalf of God but was not at all God himself? Or was the figure there considered to be an angel and God at the same time?

The word "angel" means messenger. This person couldn't be God because he is a messenger from God. On the other hand, he can't just be an angel because he speaks as God all the way through the passage. He even refers to himself as "I AM THAT I AM" in verse 14. There could be no higher claim to divinity than that. Moses seemed to have believed in Him, as he took off his shoes to acknowledge the holiness of the place.

The exact same dynamic takes place at the crossing of the Red Sea. This time the mysterious figure is not in a burning bush but in a pillar of fire and cloud. At one moment the person is called an angel, and the next moment he is called YHVH.

**Exodus 13:21—And YHVH went before them in a pillar of cloud by day... and a pillar of fire by night.**

**Exodus 14:19—And the angel of YHVH went before the camp of Israel... and the pillar of cloud went before them...**

**Exodus 14:24—And YHVH looked out upon the camp of Egypt from the pillar of fire and cloud.**

In 13:21 and in 14:24 the Torah declares that this was YHVH in the pillar. In 14:19, the Torah says that this was the angel of YHVH. So who was it? How can a person be at the same time both an angel and YHVH?

At one point this mysterious figure actually removes some of the cloud from around him and lets seventy-four of the leaders of Israel see him directly.

**Exodus 24:10–12**

**Then Moses went up and also Aaron, Nadav and Abihu, and seventy of the elders of Israel. And they saw the God of Israel. And there was under His feet as it were a paved work of sapphire stone... But He did not put His hand forth on the nobles of Israel. So they saw God, and they ate and drank.**

This is astonishing. We have always been told that it is impossible to see God, and that God could never have the form of a human. But here many people saw Him. In both verse 10 and 12 it is repeated that they saw God. The word for God here is Elohim. They saw Elohim.

This passage also states that they saw his feet. The word in Hebrew is actually legs. The one whom they saw had a human-like form. And they ate in His presence to confirm the fact that this encounter was real. It was not their imagination. This encounter with God was so real that the Torah records that the mere fact they were not killed was extraordinary.

At the burning bush, at the Red Sea and on Mount Sinai, there was a unique figure who is described sometimes as a man, sometimes as an angel, sometimes as God, and sometimes as Elohim.

## To Joshua

This exceptional person also appeared to Joshua, and in another slightly different form. Here Joshua is alone in the field the night before the battle of Jericho and has this unusual encounter.

### Joshua 5:13-15

**When Joshua was by Jericho, he lifted up his eyes and behold, a man stood opposite him with his sword drawn in his hand. And Joshua went to him and said, "Are you for us or for our adversaries?"**

**But he said, "No, I have come now as the commander of the army of YHVH." And Joshua fell on his face to the earth and worshiped, and said to him, "What does my Lord say to his servant?"**

**Then the commander of the army of YHVH said to Joshua, "Take your sandal off your foot, for the place where you stand is holy." And Joshua did so.**

There is a "man" who comes to Joshua (v. 13). He is a man; yet he is the commander of YHVH's army. That army is made up of warrior angels. So this person is an angel, or at least the commander of the angels. But then Joshua calls him Lord and bows down to him.

This commander of the angelic armies also tells him to take his shoes off, because the place where he stands is holy. That statement indicates that the person who met with Joshua was claiming to be the same one who met with Moses in the burning bush. And the one in the burning bush was YHVH, the God of Israel.

Joshua sees him clearly and talks to him openly as a man, and then worships him as God. How can this be? Who can this be? Whoever it is, he combines in one person the attributes of God and man, of YVHV and an angel. In any case, he is the one who led Joshua into the battle of Jericho.

## To Ezekiel

The puzzle becomes even more intense when we come to the prophet Ezekiel. His encounter is so extraordinary that there is a warning from rabbinic sages not even to read about it (Talmud Bavli, Chagigah 14 B).

Ezekiel saw the glory of God; he saw the cherubim and the chariot. He saw fire and lightning and the wheels turning within the wheels. It was the greatest vision any man ever had of the God of Israel. Ezekiel chapter one describes this vision in detail.

Above the cloud of glory was the firmament, like a sea of crystal that forms the divider between heaven and earth in the spiritual realm. On top of that firmament, above the glory cloud and the cherubim, was a chair, a throne.

**Ezekiel 1:26-27**

**Above the firmament over their heads was the likeness of a chair, in appearance like a sapphire stone. On the likeness of the chair was the likeness of the appearance of a man from above.**

**And from the appearance of his waist and upward I saw like electric color and the appearance of fire. I saw this appearance of fire shining all around him.**

No wonder the rabbis warned against this. The vision is absolutely explosive. The glory of God looks like the mushroom cloud of a nuclear bomb. There are supernatural creatures, the heavens open, the mystical chariot of God, and at the very center of this glory was a chair. The word for chair in Hebrew is the same as the word for throne. On this throne of glory was a man! Or at least someone who looked like a man. He was not an ordinary man, but a man with the nuclear power and fire emanating from him.

Is this God? Or is it a man? Or is it God who looks like a man? It is almighty God who appears in glory with the form of a man. It is that God-Man that the rabbis were trying to conceal from our people. If you understand what Ezekiel saw, either you will believe in Him or it will drive you crazy. In either case you can't stay neutral.

## To Daniel

The prophet Daniel saw a mysterious man receiving power and authority over the nations of the world.

### Daniel 7:13-14

**I saw in the night visions, and behold, there came with the clouds of heaven, one who was like a son of man. He was brought before the Ancient of days and came up to Him. Dominion and glory and a kingdom were given to him. And all the peoples, nations and tongues worshiped him. His dominion will be eternal and not be taken away; and his kingdom will not come to an end.**

Here are actually two figures. One is sitting on a throne and the other is brought standing in front of Him. The one sitting is called the Ancient of days. We can only assume that He is God our heavenly Father, the eternal creator. But who is this other person?

He is described as being "like" a human being. In some ways he could be called a human, but in other ways not. He is given governing authority over all the nations of the world. All the peoples serve him and worship him. His government is not just a political entity, but an eternal kingdom.

His kingdom is not formed by an earthly political struggle. Rather he is given governing authority directly from God in heaven in a spiritual way. And his kingdom will not be temporary, but will last forever. It is both a government and a spiritual kingdom. Who can this special king be?

He is the one who has become the center of both Jewish and Christian faith. He is the Messiah. It remains only to determine his identity.

## The Mystery Man

Jewish people have had an aversion to Yeshua, known in the Christian world as Jesus. There are many reasons for that; partly from our sins, partly from the sins of Christians, and partly from the lies of people who were neither Christian nor Jews. Yet one of the deepest reasons has been the very thought that a person could be both God and man at the same time. That idea seems so hard to fathom, so impossible, so "un-Jewish."

However, it is the experience of our patriarchs and prophets that determines what it means to be Jewish. They wrote the Bible, and from there we gain our understanding of who God is and what He wants from us. In those Scriptures we find a figure who appears as God in the form of a man. He appeared to many of our forefathers throughout the history of ancient Israel.

The Hebrew Bible does indeed describe someone whose attributes are a combination of divine and human. The fact that He has been so vociferously rejected by our religious leaders only goes to show how unique this individual is. There are already people in every tribe and nation who believe in Him.

He was the son of David, a Jew, and a Sabra Israeli on the human side. On the divine side, he had the same qualities we just read about in the encounters with Abraham and Jacob and Moses and Joshua and Ezekiel and Daniel. And there are many other examples. How would you call someone who had the attributes of both God and a man? Someone who was sent from God like an angel, yet spoke with the authority of God Himself?

The Bible calls him the Messiah, the Son of God (**Ps. 2:2-9**). His name is Yeshua. It is a Hebrew name that means, "God Saves." He is no more or less God than the mysterious man our forefathers met. He has both human and divine qualities. It is the same person. It is the same faith. He is Yeshua. He is the solution to the mystery.

# Appendices

*Appendix One*

**Reference List**

**Divine Appearances in the Hebrew Scriptures**


| Genesis 3:8 | Elohim Yehovah walking in the Garden |
|---|---|
| Genesis 7:16 | God shuts the door of Noah's ark |
| Genesis 11:5 | God came down to see the Tower of Babel |
| Genesis 12:7 | Yehovah is seen unto Abraham |
| Genesis 15:1 | Abraham sees and hears Word-Yehovah in Person |
| Genesis 16:7 | Angel Yehovah finds Hagar fleeing |
| Genesis 17:1 | Yehovah is seen unto Abraham |
| Genesis 18:1 | Yehovah in the form of a man visits Abraham at Mamre along with two angels and spends the day with him |
| Genesis 22:15 | Angel Yehovah intervenes at the sacrifice of Isaac |
| Genesis 26:2 | Yehovah is seen unto Isaac at Gerar |
| Genesis 26:24 | Yehovah is seen unto Isaac at night in Beer Sheva |
| Genesis 28:13 | Yehovah stands on the ladder above Jacob in dream |
| Genesis 31:10 | The Angel of Elohim, the God of Beth El, appears to Jacob in dream about sheep |
| Genesis 32:25 | Man wrestles all night with Jacob at Peniel |
| Genesis 35:9 | Elohim, El Shaddai, is seen unto Jacob |
| Genesis 48:3 | Jacob tells Joseph of El Shaddai's appearance at Beth El |
| Exodus 3:2 | Angel Yehovah is seen unto Moses in burning bush; called Yehovah in verse 4, and Elohim in verse 15 |
| Exodus 4:24 | Yehovah tries to kill Moses for not circumcising his son |

| | |
|---|---|
| Exodus 13:21 | Yehovah goes before them in pillar of cloud; called the Angel of Elohim in 14:19; called Yehovah in 14:24 |
| Exodus 17:6 | Yehovah stands on the rock to bring out water |
| Exodus 24:10 | Seventy-four leaders of Israel see the God of Israel on the Mount; called Elohim in verse 11 |
| Exodus 33:9 | Yehovah comes down to stand at door of tent of meeting |
| Numbers 11:25 | Yehovah comes down to give Holy Spirit |
| Numbers 22:22 | Angel Yehovah comes to Balaam on donkey; called Elohim in verse 9; called Yehovah in verse 28 |
| Deuteronomy 31:5 | Yehovah appears at tabernacle in cloud to Moses and Joshua |
| Joshua 5:13 | Man with sword drawn stands before Joshua on eve of Jericho; called Commander of Yehovah's Army in verse 14; on holy ground in verse 15 |
| Judges 2:1 | Angel Yehovah comes up to Gilgal to visit Israelites |
| Judges 6:12 | Angel Yehovah is seen unto Gideon; called Yehovah in verse 14 |
| Judges 13:3 | Angel Yehovah is seen unto Manoah's wife; called Elohim in verse 22 |
| 1 Samuel 3:10 | Yehovah stands next to Samuel's bed; called Yehovah's Word in verse 7 |
| 1 Kings 3:5 | Yehovah is seen unto Solomon in dream at Gibeon (2 Chron. 1:7) |
| 1 Kings 9:2 | Yehovah is seen unto Solomon a second time (2 Chron. 7:12) |
| 1 Kings 22:19 | Micayhu sees Yehovah sitting on throne |
| 1 Kings 19:7 | Angel Yehovah makes lunch for Elijah; called Angel in verse 5 |
| 2 Kings 1:3 | Angel Yehovah speaks to Elijah |
| 2 Kings 1:15 | Angel Yehovah speaks to Elijah again |

| | |
|---|---|
| 1 Chronicles 21:16 | Angel Yehovah stands between heaven and earth with sword drawn before David at Araunah's threshing floor (2 Sam. 24:16) |
| Job 1:6 | Sons of God and Satan come before Yehovah |
| Job 2:1 | Sons of God and Satan come before Yehovah |
| Job 38:1 | Yehovah appears to Job in whirlwind |
| Isaiah 6: 1 | Isaiah sees Adonai sitting on throne, called Yehovah of Armies in verse 3; called King Yehovah of Armies in verse 5 |
| Isaiah 37:36 | Angel Yehovah kills 180,000 Assyrians in one night after Hezekiah's prayer (2 Kings 19:35) |
| Ezekiel 1:26 | Ezekiel sees one like a man sitting on a throne on top of the glory and cherubim. |
| Ezekiel 3:23 | Ezekiel sees glory second time |
| Ezekiel 8:2 | Ezekiel sees man of fire and glory a third time, called Adonai Yehovah in verse 1 |
| Ezekiel 10:1-3 | Ezekiel sees man on glory throne a fourth time |
| Ezekiel 43:2-7 | Ezekiel sees man on glory throne a fifth time |
| Ezekiel 44-46 | The exalted Prince enters the Millennial Temple |
| Daniel 3:25 | Nebuchadnezzar sees a fourth man in furnace as Son of God |
| Daniel 7:13 | One like the Son of Man brought before the Ancient of Days |
| Daniel 10:5 | Daniel sees Man with fire |
| Amos 7:7 | Amos sees Adonai standing next to wall with plumb line in hand |
| Amos 9:1 | Amos sees Adonai standing next to altar |
| Zechariah 1:11-12 | Angel Yehovah standing among myrtle trees |
| Zechariah 3:1 | Zechariah sees Angel Yehovah standing next to Joshua the High Priest; called Yehovah in verse 2 |
| Zechariah 14:4 | Feet of Yehovah will stand on Mount of Olives |

*Appendix Two*

**The Divine Angel**

*Textual Criticism and the Forgotten Legend*

By Solomon Intrater

Recently I finished a B.A. at the Hebrew University. I majored in "Bible," meaning the Hebrew Scriptures. This field would be more accurately described as *textual criticism* of the Hebrew Scriptures. My professors were secular or religious Jewish Israeli scholars. Their approach to Scripture is of course very different from traditional Christianity and Judaism. Some of them still believe in God and cherish the Israelite heritage, without recognizing Scripture as authored by divine inspiration but rather the traditions of man.

*Textual Criticism* is very different than *Theology*. Theology takes Scripture as given, assuming that the Scriptures are complete and perfect, and then develops theory to describe God in a consistent manner based on Scripture. Though Textual Criticism is definitely not void of subjectivity (theology, culture, character and personal experience), it is more technical and is concerned with the text itself. Theology is irrelevant. The text is not assumed complete and perfect. The texts of the Hebrew Bible are analyzed and questioned.

I chose to write my thesis on the Angel of YHVH because my father preached about this character often, and I had been looking into it myself. In my paper, I compared the appearances of the term *malach yhvh* (Angel-YHVH) or *malach ha'elohim* (Angel of God). In English Bibles, the one original Hebrew term is translated in many different ways [such as: the Angel of the LORD, the divine messenger, an angel of the LORD, a messenger of God]. Thus the original textual linkage is prone to be lost in translation, which is dangerous for correct interpretation. I compared the various appearances of this specific term, and analyzed various forms of textual linkage, such as similar functions, traits, terminology and quotations.

The thesis was to suggest that most of these appearances were dealing with one specific individual. A different approach could be that in each case it is a different angel, different kinds of angels, arbitrary angels. The difficulty is that the text itself in Hebrew does not literally differentiate between definite or indefinite: it could be literally translated as an angel of the LORD or the Angel of the LORD.

Another difficulty is that in many of these cases such an entity is of divine character, or is related to as God, or performs a divine function. There are different textual explanations: the various stories are taken from ancient literature from the surrounding religions where gods are not amorphous and they interact and are seen by men; the different stories in the Bible originated from different independent sources and traditions; the original text was tampered with and edited changing God to an angel in order to distort the old theology of God who was not amorphous and was seen and did interact with man; the original text was tampered with and edited in order to distort the angels and make them God Himself because they were seen as heretical to monotheism.

The thesis begins from an impression reading the story of Manoach's wife and the angel in Judges 13. She is visited in the field by an individual. She tells her husband Manoach. Together they are suspicious of this individual: "the man of God came to me his countenance was like the countenance of *malach ha'elohim*, very awesome! I did not question him where he was from and he did not tell me his name..." (v. 6). These Israelites encounter an individual, and they wonder if he is indeed the particular individual whose legend they and their people are familiar with. Manoach prays to God to send this individual a second time and this prayer is answered. After the angel repeats his message to Manoach, the events take a turn from verse 15 onwards: they question him, they invite him to stay, and they offer to make a sacrifice to him. It's as if they are now confident that this individual is indeed *the* one. In response to their curiosity regarding his identity, the angel ascends in the midst of the flame and disappears. Then, verse 21 states "then Manoach knew that he (the visitor) was indeed *malach-YHVH*." The couple falls to their faces in fear because they have seen God.

My impression from Judges 13 is that the people of Israel in the land of Israel, following the history of the Exodus and the inheritance of the Land, are *familiar with the tradition of the great divine angel*. When they are met by the visitor, they think of the *legend they are already familiar with*. After the visitor said what he said and did what he did, they were then sure that this indeed was the one.

Today in religious tradition *this character is somewhat forgotten*. Nobody speaks of him, no one is aware of him. But in the text, the people *are* familiar with this character. Who is he? What is he? Is such an individual really recurrent and recognized in the Israelite tradition in the Bible? I continued to read the critical approach of the professors in the department. I discovered that they themselves professed that indeed there was some sort of a tradition that is forgotten yet embedded within the text. This is the tradition of a particular divine messenger who played a part in many of the events in the Bible, such as the Exodus and the inheritance of the Land. And this entity is divine in some way.

The conclusion was that in many of these cases, it is legitimate to interpret the text as referring to a specific and definite individual; also that there is much textual linkage between the various appearances of this term/character *malach-YHVH*. The text suggests that within the Israelite tradition there was an understanding and recognition of this particular entity. If we assume these different appearances speak of the same person, then we can construct his character and function: God yet not God himself (the distinction is often obscure), appears in the form of man, carries God's name and authority, often functions as a "savior" or "redeemer"—one who rescues, also one who leads, brings news, fights and punishes.

*Note: subtle references to the tradition of the Angel of YHVH in biblical poetry, prayer, prophecy and conversation: Genesis 48:16, Judges 5:23, 1 Samuel 29:9, 2 Samuel 14:17 & 20, 19:28, Psalm 34:8, 35:5, Zechariah 12:8.

## *Appendix Three*
## Yehovah and Yahweh

Words have great spiritual importance. God created the world with words, and rules over the world with words. The power of words is in their meaning, not so much in their pronunciation. I am often asked how the name of YHVH is pronounced (Yahweh or Yehovah). The very question partly misses the point. There is no discussion in the Torah, the Prophets or the New Covenant on how to pronounce the name.

A name is a word that describes a person. The names in the Bible had prophetic meaning. They described a person's character, his destiny, his purpose. To the degree that we are looking at a name to have power by its sounds, we have fallen into superstition. However, when we seek to understand the spiritual significance of a name, we are touching the root of its power.

So if I were asked how to pronounce the name YHVH, I would like to respond:

**Exodus 34:5-7**
**And YHVH came down in a cloud and stood with him there and called upon the name YHVH. And YHVH crossed before His face and cried, "YHVH, merciful God and gracious, longsuffering and great in mercy and truth, keeping mercy to thousands…"**

Thus the Angel YHVH declared to Moses the name and the meaning of the name on Mount Sinai. This is His full name, as it were, a list of character qualities. It was not a lesson on pronunciation; it was an explanation of God's attributes and "personhood." This same Angel had earlier said to Moses:

**Exodus 6:3**
**I appeared to Abraham, to Isaac and to Jacob as El Shaddai but by My name YHVH I was not known to them.**

This statement does not mean that the people of Israel did not know of the name YHVH, nor how to pronounce it. It means that they had not received the full meaning of the name as it was revealed to them during the Exodus and at Sinai. Again the issue here is not one of pronunciation, but of revelation. We know this because the letters and sound of the name were already known to mankind long before this, even at the time of Enosh.

**Genesis 4:26**
**Then men began to call upon the name of YHVH.**

The early patriarchs knew how to call on the name YHVH, but they did not have the fullness of the meaning of that name. The revelation they had was of the meaning of the name El or Elohim. The root of the word in Hebrew for El means "power." The patriarchs knew God as El Shaddai, the God of nature, provision, power and protection.

At the time of Moses, the people of Israel received more revelation of God, concerning His judgment, redemption, and holiness. That's what they learned at the Exodus—not a different way of pronouncing the letters.

The root of the name YHVH in Hebrew means "to be." The letter V may well have been pronounced more like the sound W in ancient times. However, between the V or W pronunciation there is no difference in meaning, and therefore virtually no significance, in my opinion.

Biblical Hebrew was written only in consonants, as we see in the letters YHVH. Therefore the main question of pronunciation concerns which vowel (points) to add to the consonants. The vowels can make a difference in the meaning. If we add the vowels— "e" — "o"— "a"—to the consonants, we receive the name YeHoVah.

In this format, the "e" (*sh'va*) stands for the future tense, the "o" (*holom*) for the present tense, and the "a" (*patach*) refers to the past tense. That gives meaning to the name YeHoVah as "He will be, He is, He was." In other words, the Eternal One. This meaning fits the understanding of the early partriarchs.

Many scholars choose the pronunciation, YaHWeH, as representing the "causative" form in the Hebrew, meaning "he who caused existence." This is a possibility. However, there are other grammatical reasons that make YeHoVaH preferable in my view.

Hebrew vowels change form depending on the number of syllables, and on where the syllables are located in the name. If there is just one syllable, such as Yah, then the "a" vowel is correct. Or if the letters come at the end of the word, such as Eliyah (Elijah), then the "a" is also correct. Yet, when the vowel comes at the beginning with multiple syllables, it changes. This can easily be proved by checking a concordance of the Bible.

Such names as Yehoyachin or Yehoshua or Yehoyada or Yehoshaphat contain the same root letters as YHVH, in the same syllable arrangement. All of the names in this pattern display the vowels as "e"— "o"— "a." If that same pattern is placed in the letters YHVH, we see the name again as Yehovah. There is not one example in the Hebrew Scriptures of a three syllable name containing the root YHVH that does not use the vowel pattern of "e" — "o"—"a."

Since EVERY example of the YHVH root used in biblical names in this pattern shows the vowels as "e" — "o" — "a," one would have to show some other overwhelming evidence, textually or grammatically, to choose a different pronunciation. There is no such other overwhelming documentation weighty enough to refute the biblical and grammatical evidence.

In summary, 1) the meaning of the vowels, 2) the grammatical form and 3) the list of biblical examples, all point to Yehovah (or Yehowah) as the preferred pronunciation over Yahweh.

Pronunciation of the name, for mere pronunciation sake makes little difference. If it were an important issue, Yeshua or one of the apostles would have emphasized it. Religious cults in both the Jewish and Christian worlds have at times placed great emphasis on certain pronunciations, but that emphasis cannot be supported in Scripture.

(For example: it is popular among some ultra orthodox Jewish rabbis in Jerusalem today to refer to YHVH as "D" [*daleth*]. Another rabbinic tradition holds that Yeshua performed miracles by "stealing" the pronunciation of the name YHVH from the Holy of Holies, writing it on a note and inserting it in His thigh [*Toldot Yeshu,* chapter 3].)

This pronunciation issue carries over into the name of Yeshua Himself. The name Yeshua is a shortened form of Yehoshua (Joshua). Yehoshua itself is a contraction of the words Yehovah Yoshia (Yehovah Saves). In other words, the name YHVH is contained INSIDE the name of Yeshua. This corresponds to the biblical prophecy:

**Exodus 23:20-21**
**Behold I send an Angel before you to keep you in the way... Be careful of Him and hear His voice... for My name is inside Him.**

What an amazing prophecy: the name of YHVH would be contained in the name of the Angel who would lead the children of Israel. This Angel YHVH would have the power, character and authority of the name of YHVH. In addition, the name of YHVH would be contained in the Angel's name. Both dimensions of this prophecy were fulfilled when Yeshua received His name at birth.

Some Christians and Messianic Jews today want to spell the Messiah's name as Y'shua or Yahshua, while many modern Israelis refer to Him as Yeshu.

All of those pronunciations are patently incorrect. The name Yeshua is found thirty times in the Hebrew text of the post exilic history books of the Bible (like Ezra and Nehemiah).

Every single time the name is written Yeshua. The vowel point is a *tsere*, not a *patach*, *kamats* or *sh'va*; not even a *segol*. There is always an *ayin* at the end of the name. One could make an argument for transliterating the name as Yeishu'a, but certainly not Y'shua, Yahshua or Yeshu.

Personally, I don't care how someone pronounces His name. I only want to help my friends not to be taken captive by someone with a cultic, hypocritical or phony intellectual spirit, telling you that you are wrong if you don't pronounce it just the way they say (even when what they are telling you is not the correct pronunciation anyway). By contrast the seven Skeva brothers all pronounced the name of Yeshua perfectly, yet missed the meaning and authority of the name, and thus were overcome by Satan (**Acts 19:14**).

There is revelatory meaning to the name Yeshua. The name and authority of YHVH is found INSIDE that name. You don't have to worry about how to pronounce YHVH, because YHVH is already contained in Yeshua. Or to rephrase an old advertising slogan, "When you've said Yeshua, you've said it all."

I would summarize the revelation of the divine names this way: "El" stands for God's power; "Yehovah" stands for His holiness, and "Yeshua" stands for His love. Those are the three general attributes of God: power, holiness and love. God revealed His name (His character qualities) to mankind in three great progressive revelations. God was known first as Elohim. Then He was known better as Yehovah. Now He can be known in Yeshua.

## *Appendix Four*
## Yehovah and Yeshua

In Appendix #3, we discussed the difference between the pronunciations of the name Yahweh and Yehovah, as well as the reasons for using the name Yeshua. Here are a few points as to the connection between the name Yehovah and Yeshua (Jesus).

1.  **Power:** There was great power and authority in the declaration of the name YHVH (Yehovah) by our forefathers in the days of the Law and the Prophets.

2.  **Not Generic:** This power was not associated with generic names, such as Lord, God, Adonai, Hashem, but only in the proper name Yehovah.

3.  **Unknown:** Today we do not know exactly how to pronounce the name Yehovah, and therefore in the Jewish community, it is forbidden. As the name is not declared, there is a lack of the power and authority that goes with it.

4.  **Sovereignty:** This "forgetting" of the pronunciation of the YHVH in the Jewish community cannot simply be a coincidence. It is a sovereign intervention of God to bring about a new situation.

5.  **Yehovah inside Yeshua:** The name Yeshua is a shortened form of Yehoshua, which is a shortened form of Yehovah Yoshiah— "The Lord saves." In other words, the name Yehovah is found INSIDE the name Yeshua.

6.  **Saying Yeshua is Saying Yehovah:** Therefore, when we say the name Yeshua, we are already saying the name of Yehovah, and even more. When you say Yeshua, you are pronouncing the awesome name Yehovah as well.

7.  **No Other Name:** At this moment in history, there is no other way to pronounce the name of Yehovah with power and authority, other than saying Yeshua. This gives insight to **Acts 4:12**— **"There is no salvation in another; for there is no other name given to the sons of men under the heavens by which we are to be saved."**

8. **No name, No Power:** If we do not say Yeshua, we cannot have the power that was originally present in the name Yehovah.

9. **Same Power:** However, when we do say the name Yeshua (and do so with faith and understanding and according to God's will), we are releasing the same power and authority that our forefathers did when they said Yehovah.

10. **Continuance:** The name Yeshua is the continuance in our day and era of what the name Yehovah was in the day and era of our forefathers.

11. **Same Attitude:** Therefore our attitude, approach and respect for the name Yeshua is the same as our forefathers had for the name Yehovah.

12. **Messianic Gift:** We in the Messianic Jewish movement want to restore to Israel and to the international body of Messiah the name of Yeshua—not just the original pronunciation of the name, but the original power and authority of the name. The name Yeshua contains the name of Yehovah within it and all of the spiritual revelations and manifestations that go along with that name—and even more. There is authority in the name Yeshua in all three dimensions— "heaven, earth and under the earth" (**Phil. 2:9**).

## *Appendix Five*
## Keeping the Sabbath

When sharing the gospel in Israel, we have to deal with the question of whether we "keep the commandments." When religious Jews say, "commandments," they mix together the biblical commandments and the added rabbinic commandments. If we say "No," we have lost the authority of the Scriptures. If we say "Yes," they ask about which *halacha* (rabbinic laws) we keep.

Our answer to this question has to be an unequivocal "Yes," but then immediately explain that we have a different method of doing so. The first difference is that we accept biblical commandments as authoritative, but not rabbinic commandments. When I explained this on Israeli television, the interviewer readily understood our position. The discussion then opened up into many deeper issues. (He thought we were like the Karaites, an ancient sect of Judaism which receives Scriptures as authoritative, but not halacha.)

### Original Context

Biblical commandments, which were given several thousand years ago, cannot be fulfilled in a vacuum. The commandments were given as part of a four-fold set:

1. The Angel of YHVH (who wrote the Ten Commandments on Mount Sinai)

2. The commandments themselves (with different levels of importance; Matt. 23:23)

3. The blood sacrifices (which provided forgiveness when laws were transgressed)

4. The Holy Spirit (to guide and empower the people to fulfill the Law; Num. 11:25-29; Rom. 8:2-4)

As Messianic Jews we have come to understand that the Angel of the Lord is often Yeshua (Jesus), that the commandments of love and morality supersede those of ritual symbolism, that the crucifixion of Yeshua has given the full meaning to the sacrifices, and that the Holy Spirit has come to dwell inside us. This perspective gives balance to applying the commandments in our daily life of faith.

In the New Covenant the law has been written on our hearts (Jer. 31:31); therefore our method of keeping commandments is internally motivated, with emphasis on the "heart" meaning of the commandments, and much flexibility concerning external details of ritual.

Rabbinic Judaism endeavors to keep the commandments, but has taken them out of context. The Torah itself remains the same. However, halachic laws replace the leading of the Holy Spirit, the rabbis replace the Messiah, and blood atonement is generally missing.

One of my sons was recently sharing with a religious Jew, and when asked whether we keep the commandments, he said, "Yes, but we have a different way of applying them." He came home and reported, "Dad, this really worked to open a serious discussion on the true meaning of faith and the Messiah."

### Sabbath Laws

The base of all moral commandments is the Ten Commandments. The Ten Commandments are found in three places in the Torah: Exodus 20, Leviticus 19, and Deuteronomy 5—all in slightly different forms. The commandment that causes the most argument is the Sabbath. Rabbinic Judaism can be obsessive at times regarding Sabbath laws. For example, there is a disagreement as to whether it is allowable to tear toilet paper on the Sabbath—and therefore some groups use toilet paper "pre-separated" into small sections for the Sabbath.

[Once, my friend Joe Shulam was teaching on Talmud and came across a passage which indicated that the sin of the golden calf took place on the Shabbat. An elderly religious Jewish woman in attendance called out, "No that couldn't be!" Joe asked her why. She replied, "They were Jews weren't they?" In recounting this story, Joe and I laughed so hard we cried. I guess you have to be Jewish to "get" the joke. Her point was: adultery, idolatry, occult, and rebellion—that's understandable; but break the Sabbath—God forbid!]

### Yeshua's Sabbath Laws

There are thousands of pages of rabbinic literature about Sabbath laws. Yeshua summarized His halacha in three simple rules:

**Mark 2:27—The Sabbath was made for man.**

Yeshua returns to the original purpose of the Sabbath. It was designed to be a weekly release from the curse of the sin of Adam. It was to be a taste of the millennial kingdom to come. It was a time to rest from the things of this world and turn our hearts to the Lord.

### Mark 2:28—The Son of Man is Lord of the Sabbath.

Yeshua refers to Himself as the final authority of how to keep the Sabbath. It was He in the form of the Angel/YHVH who wrote the Sabbath commandment in the first place. The rabbis say that it is impossible to keep commandments without supervision. Everyone needs a rabbi to instruct how to fulfill the details. If you have a rabbi's instruction, then you will have no doubts of whether you have acted correctly. Yeshua is our rabbi, and we fulfill the Sabbath according to His instructions.

### Mark 3:4—It is lawful to do good on the Sabbath.

Yeshua reiterates that moral law overrides ritual law. He reminds us that correct interpretation of the law demands simple morality, logical discernment, and a healthy approach to human life.

I reject the position that traditional Jews keep the commandments and Messianic Jews do not. We do keep God's commandments, but seek to do so by restoring their original meaning in the light of the New Covenant. Much of Christianity has dismissed the commandments of God by theological excuses; much of Judaism has distorted the commandments of God by ritual traditions.

*Appendix Six*
## Ladder of Gospel and Law

In 2009, the Messianic Jewish Alliance of Israel sponsored a national assembly of pastors and elders in which the role of Jewish tradition in our teachings and congregations was debated. Some were for; others were against. I endeavored to share a balancing viewpoint by setting a ladder of priorities in our understanding.

The relationship between the Gospel message and Jewish tradition can be described in a simple way by imagining a ladder of four rungs or priorities:

1. Salvation by grace
2. Moral law
3. Ritual law
4. Religious tradition

### Salvation by Grace

Yeshua (Jesus) took our punishment on the cross and then rose from the dead to provide eternal life. That message is more important than anything else. We are beings created by a loving and holy God. We have sinned. All righteousness comes from Him. Without trusting in His righteousness, no human being can hope to become righteous on his own. That is a central theme of the book of Romans.

### Moral Law

For that reason, salvation by grace is more important than the moral Law. Yet moral standards are essential. And who establishes what those standards are? Only a person who himself is perfectly righteous. Therefore, moral standards must come from God alone. God's moral standards are absolute and valid to all human beings. They are written in the Bible. The most succinct list of His moral code is the Ten Commandments. (See **Matt. 19:17.**)

Within the Law are commandments of greater importance, and those of lesser. Yeshua exhorted us not to **"forsake the weightier matters of the Law—justice, mercy and faith"**—**Matthew 23:23.** In order to obey God's commandments, we have to understand which aspects are more important, and which are less.

## Ritual Law

The basic division between what is primary and what is secondary is between the moral law (love) and the ritual law (symbols). **"To love God with all your heart and all your understanding and all your might, and to love your neighbor as yourself, behold, is greater than all sacrifice and offering."** (Mark 12:23)

Ritual laws or "signs" of the covenant are not binding commandments in the same way that the moral commandments are. **"Neither circumcision nor uncircumcision is important, but rather keeping the commandments of God."** (1 Cor. 7:19) Isn't circumcision a commandment? Yes, in the sense that it is part of the ritual law recorded in the Bible. No, in the sense that it is not part of the absolute moral law.

Circumcision, festivals, and food laws are not on the same level as the commandments against lying, stealing, adultery and murder. Not recognizing the priority of moral law over ritual law is a critical misunderstanding of the Law itself, and may result in religious hypocrisy. Yeshua rebuked the Pharisees for misinterpreting and therefore disobeying the Law. **"Woe to you, blind guides, who strain a gnat and swallow a camel."** (Matt. 23:24) (Unfortunately, much of the Christian world has rejected the Law altogether, often resulting in sin and moral transgression even by those who preach the gospel.)

## Religious Tradition

The ritual aspects of Jewish law may be divided themselves into two sections: those which are biblical, and those which are additions from the rabbis. The symbols in the Bible are specifically ordained by God with a spiritual message concerning His kingdom plan. Those added by the rabbis are a matter of culture and have no direct authority.

Elevating tradition to the status of divine law is extremely dangerous. Yeshua referred to this as **"the learned commandment of men"** (quoting **Isa. 29:13**), and asked, **"Why do you disobey the commandment of God for the sake of your own traditions?"** (Matt. 15:3) Equating religious tradition to the Law of God is an evil found in all religion, whether Jewish, Christian or pagan.

Religious tradition is never binding. However, when we share the good news of salvation, we should embrace in love the culture of the people group we are sharing with. This is particularly true of the Jewish people, who developed a religious culture based on Old Testament (*Tenach*). **"For the sake of the**

**Jews, I am as a Jew in order to win them** (for salvation); **for the sake of those under the Law, I am as one under the Law."** (1 Cor. 9:20)

In summary:
1. The message of salvation through Yeshua is our highest priority
2. Good works of human origin cannot save us
3. God's absolute moral law is binding for all human beings
4. Moral law is higher than ritual law
5. Biblical symbols or rituals point to spiritual kingdom truths
6. Religious tradition is never binding or authoritative
7. Elevating religious tradition to moral law is a dangerous error
8. Embracing someone else's culture in love may be an important bridge in sharing with them eternal life

**Apples of Gold**

Think of this biblical parable: **"Apples of gold in settings of silver is a word spoken in its fashions" (Prov. 25:11).** What we have to say is compared to a golden apple. How we say it is compared to fittings of silver. We in the Messianic movement have often been so concerned with the Jewish form of what we have to say, that we miss the center of the message itself. Our Jewish culture and identity is not the message. Sometimes we have offered a silver setting without the golden apple.

On the other hand, the setting is important. If a Frenchman wanted to give an Englishman a fish, he might write on the box "poisson" (French for "fish"). However, the Englishman would undoubtedly think it was "poison." Often well-meaning Christians have tried to bring the "fish" of eternal life to our people, yet our people see it as poison.

We want to have the right message and the right manner of expression; the right content in the right context: the gospel of Yeshua in its Jewish historical setting.

## Appendix Seven
## Restoration of All Things

We believe in the biblical principle of restoration. God made everything in the world "very good" (**Gen. 1:31**). Yet, Adam's sin and Satan's rebellion caused much destruction. God's plan of redemption not only saves us from damnation, it also restores the damage that was caused.

That restoration is first personal. Our spirit; soul and body are redeemed. However, God's restoration is also general, and includes everything in the world. Personal restoration is better known in the Christian world, while world restoration is better known in the Jewish world. The New Covenant includes both.

The traditional Jewish prayer, *Aleinu* (*It is incumbent upon us*), which closes every service, three times per day, makes a petition— לתקן עולם במלכות שדי — "to repair the world in the kingdom of El Shaddai." The word here for "repair" is— תיקון —*Tikkun*. [This is the name we use for our cooperative ministries with Dan Juster, Don Finto, David Rudolph, Eitan Shishkoff and Paul Wilbur.]

World restoration (*Tikkun*) is central not only to our ministry, but to the worldview of the kingdom of God. There are five passages in the New Covenant that speak specifically of world restoration.

1. **Matthew 17**: The Church
2. **Romans 11**: The Messianic remnant
3. **Matthew 19**: Natural Creation
4. **Acts 1**: Kingdom of Israel
5. **Acts 3**: All Things

### Matthew 17:11
### Elijah is coming first and will restore all things.

Yeshua prophesies that someone in the spirit and power of Elijah will come "first" —that means, before Yeshua returns. The "days of Elijah" restoration will take place before the 2nd Coming. The phrase, "all things" cannot mean all things in the world, because that will only happen after Yeshua returns. This restoration is parallel to the prophecy that "the bride will make herself ready" (Rev. 19:7). The elements of the kingdom of God will be restored within the community of faith before Yeshua returns. When He returns, what is within the people of God will be revealed and given to the nations. A central theme of prophetic ministry in our generation is the restoration of the true Church as we approach the 2nd Coming.

## Romans 11:15
### What will their restoration be but life from the dead?

There will also be a restoration of the Messianic remnant of Israel. This dual restoration can be seen in Revelation 7:4 and 9. The elements to be restored are those found in the early community of faith in the book of Acts. There we see sacrificial love, extravagant giving, bold evangelism, miraculous signs, and unity of the saints.

The end times remnant of Israel will be even stronger than the apostolic community of the first century (Rom. 11:12). The revival of the end times will be greater than the revival they experienced (Acts 2:17). The Messianic remnant will be a key element leading to the resurrection of the dead.

## Matthew 19:28
### In the regeneration, when the Son of Man sits on the throne of His glory, you who have followed Me will also sit on twelve thrones, judging the twelve tribes of Israel.

As both the international Church and the remnant of Israel come into their fullness (Rom. 11:15 and 25), they will together call upon Yeshua to return (Matt. 23:39; Rev. 22:20). At that time the kingdom of God will be established on the earth for 1,000 years. This Millennial kingdom will include two key elements.

The first is "regeneration." The Hebrew translation says, "renewal of creation." The Greek original is *paliggenesia—pali* means "again" and *genesia* means "genesis" like creation in the book of Genesis. Natural creation will be redeemed (Rom. 8:19-22). The heavens and earth will be renewed as they were immediately after the flood of Noah (2 Pet. 3:3-5). People will begin to live longer lives (Isa. 65:17, 20).

The second element is a worldwide kingdom with its capital in Jerusalem.

## Acts 1:6
### Will You at this time restore the kingdom to Israel?

The apostles expected Yeshua to restore the Davidic kingdom immediately upon His resurrection from the dead. However, He told them they first had to receive the Holy Spirit and preach the gospel to the nations. His kingdom was to be international, not just Israelite; and spiritual, not just governmental. It is a renewal and expansion of the Davidic kingdom (Isa. 2:2-4). The former dominion will be restored (Mic. 4:8).

Yeshua will sit upon His throne in Jerusalem; the apostles will sit on twelve thrones governing the tribes of Israel. Those who have "followed Him" will sit on thrones governing the rest of the nations—when Yeshua returns in glory (Matt. 16:27; 19:28; 24:30; 24:46-47; 25:21; 25:31; 26:64).

**Acts 3:21**
**Whom the heavens must receive until the time of the restoration of all things; which God has spoken by the mouth of all His prophets since the world began.**

Ultimately, God will restore all things. There is nothing that will not be restored. This includes everything planned at creation; everything prophesied to Israel; everything promised to the Church. It includes all things in heaven and earth (Eph. 1:10). God's commitment to restore all things is a source of great hope and encouragement to us all.

*Appendix Eight*

**Heaven and Earth**

The kingdom of God has aspects that are heavenly and aspects that are earthly. To understand the kingdom, we have to understand God's purpose for both heaven *and* earth. Let's review here a series of seven verses that contain the words "heaven and earth." (Please note them for future reference.)

**Genesis 1:1**
**In the beginning God created the heavens and the earth.**

Before God created anything, He had already **planned** the kingdom, the crucifixion, the resurrection, heaven, hell, etc. What He wanted at the end was already in His thoughts from the beginning. He created the heavens and the earth because He had a **purpose** for both.

Everything He created in both heaven and earth was good, even very good. The problems entered with the rebellion of Satan and the sin of man. Ultimately, sinful and satanic things will be removed, and the heavens and the earth redeemed to their final purpose (**Rom. 8:19-22**).

**Psalm 115:16**
**The heaven, even the heavens, are the Lord's; but the earth He has given to the children of men.**

This verse speaks of **delegation of authority**. The Lord has given mankind a long term lease on planet earth. The rabbis call this "the two floor apartment." God (and the angels) live in the apartment above; mankind in the apartment below. God often came to visit, like someone coming down a ladder or a staircase (Gen. 3:8; Gen. 18:1, 21; Gen. 28:12; Exod. 3:8). However, the keys to the lower apartment were in the hands of men.

Men do not own the earth; God does. But He has given us a lease of approximately 6,000 years. For example, I live in a rented apartment. The owner has to call me and ask permission if he wants to come visit. The keys are in my hands.

**Isaiah 65:17**
**Behold I create new heavens and a new earth; and the former shall not be remembered or come to mind.**

God promises to create a new heavens and earth. This does not mean that the current universe will go out of existence, but that God will **restore**,

**renew** and **redeem**. In the context of Isaiah 65, we see that the earth will be purified, but that the natural processes will continue, though greatly and supernaturally improved.

The difference is like from the time before the flood of Noah to after the flood of Noah, yet even more so (**2 Pet. 3:5-12**). When the book of Revelation (chapters 21-22) refers to New Heavens and Earth, it is giving additional revelation about this passage in Isaiah 65. As his custom, John gives spiritual insight to what is written in the other Hebrew prophets. He is adding a dimension to what was already said, not doing away with it.

Isaiah gave the earthly perspective; John the heavenly. We simply need to see it from both angles.

### Matthew 5:3, 5
**Blessed are the poor in spirit, for theirs is the kingdom of heaven. Blessed are the meek, for they shall inherit the earth.**

There are many injustices in the world today. Since God is both **powerful** and **moral**, He will remove the unjust elements. Those who are pure in heart will then take over what is here. Religions which do not understand the nature of the God of the Bible believe that pure hearted people will just leave this place for eternity. They do not see how God could bring justice, remove the wicked, reward the righteous and restore the earth. Therefore, they simply abandon God's good creation and leave for some other mystical, non physical, unidentified place.

This is what the Hindus and the New Agers call "Nirvana." Unfortunately, because of the separation of the Hebraic world view from Christianity, most Christians' view of the end times and the kingdom of God is closer to pagan mysticism than it is to the biblical description. Mysticism is escapism to a spirit only world; while the biblical view is both the spiritual and physical world restored by a benevolent Creator.

### Matthew 6:10
**Your kingdom come; Your will be done on earth as it is in heaven.**

The kingdom of God has an **origin**, a **direction** and a **destination**. It starts in heaven. It comes toward us. It eventually takes over the earth. The kingdom of God comes in stages. It grows from small to big; it grows from inside to outside (Matt. 13:31-33). The kingdom of God is an invasion, not an evacuation (albeit a gracious invasion, but an invasion none the less).

Yeshua left for a time to establish the authority of His kingdom, but is coming again to rule and reign (Luke 19:12). Most Christians look at salvation as fire insurance and a helicopter ticket. I see the kingdom as an ownership certificate and a government constitution. Although the Lord's Prayer above (about God's will being done on earth and His kingdom coming) is perhaps the most oft spoken prayer in the world, it doesn't seem to me that most people mean it when they say it.

It is worth noting that the Jewish prayer book ends *every* service with the prayer, *Aleinu*, which includes the words, "to restore (or, repair) the world in the kingdom of El Shaddai."

**Matthew 28:18**
**All authority has been given to Me in heaven and on earth.**

Yeshua is both God and man; therefore, He has authority on both heaven and earth. His authority in heaven stems from His divinity—His authority on earth from His humanity. The gospel is effective because of His **dual nature** and **dual authority**. He came from heaven and was born into a physical body on this earth. He was physically raised from the dead. He ascended into heaven. He will return some day as He ascended (Acts 1:11) and His feet will once again stand on the Mount of Olives (Zech. 14:4).

Not to affirm Yeshua's actual return to earth and a literal millennial reign is to mock the physical pain He suffered on the cross and to deny the purpose of the bodily resurrection. I am perplexed as to how difficult it is for many Christians to see the obvious and literal fulfillment of all the biblical promises concerning the millennial reign of Messiah. It is a dangerous position to dismiss hundreds of prophecies because they don't fit with one's denominational theology.

**Ephesians 1:10**
**In the dispensation of the fullness of the times, He might gather together in one all things in Messiah, both which are in heaven and on earth—in Him** (Yeshua).

Please compare this verse to **Colossians 1:16** which states that *all* things in heaven *and* earth were created for Yeshua and through Yeshua.

Today unfortunately there is still a separation between things in heaven and on earth. But that is not God's will. Ultimately all things both in heaven and on earth will be brought together through Yeshua the Messiah. That was His mission—to **unite heaven and earth**. There is another rabbinic tradition that says when a human being prays on earth with right spiritual intention, he unites the letters of the divine name YeHoVaH—the YH stand for heaven and the VH stand for earth.

Through Yeshua (and true spirit-filled believers with Him) the world will all be made one, both that which is in heaven and that which is on earth. And even God's name will be made one (Zech. 14:9). Don't settle for just half the kingdom. Israel has tended to see the earthly part without the heavenly; the Church has tended to see just the heavenly without the earthly. However, Yeshua is both King of Israel and Head of the Church.

Thank God, we get the "best of both worlds" —both that which is in heaven and that which is on the earth.

*Appendix Nine*

## Before the Foundation

Here is a list of references in the New Covenant that speak of God having a plan that was designed "Before the foundation of the world."

| | |
|---|---|
| Matthew 20:23 | Our places to sit in kingdom |
| Matthew 24:36 | Date of Second Coming |
| Matthew 25:34 | Paradise for the righteous |
| Matthew 25:41 | Punishment in fire for the wicked |
| John 1:2 | Yeshua as Word with God from creation |
| John 1:15 | Yeshua came from "before" His birth |
| John 8:58 | Yeshua existed before Abraham |
| John 17:5 | Yeshua and the Father sharing glory |
| John 17:24 | Yeshua and the Father sharing love |
| Acts 1:7 | Date of Second Coming |
| Acts 2:23 | Yeshua's death and resurrection |
| Acts 3:20 | Yeshua ordained for us beforehand |
| Acts 4:28 | God's purpose determined beforehand |
| Acts 17:26 | Predetermined boundaries of nations |
| Acts 17:30 | Predetermined the date of judgment day |
| Romans 1:2 | Gospel message promised |
| Romans 8:29 | Foreknew and destined to be like Yeshua |
| Romans 9:23 | Vessels of grace prepared beforehand |
| Romans 11:2 | Foreknew the people of Israel |
| Romans 16:25 | Secret revelations hidden |
| 1 Corinthians 2:7 | Mystery of our being glorified |
| Ephesians 1:4 | Chosen in Him to be blameless |
| Ephesians 1:5 | Predestined us to adoption as sons |
| Ephesians 1:9 | Purpose and plan to gather all in Yeshua |
| Ephesians 1:11 | Predestined inheritance for the elect |
| Ephesians 2:10 | Good works for us to do |
| Colossians 1:26 | Mystery hidden from ages |
| 2 Timothy 1:9 | Plan of salvation by grace in Yeshua |
| Titus 1:2 | Promise of eternal life |
| Hebrews 4:3 | God's works finished and divine rest |
| Hebrews 12:1 | Our race set before us |
| Hebrews 12:2 | Yeshua's joy after enduring cross |
| 1 Peter 1:2 | Chosen elect foreknown for sanctification |
| 1 Peter 1:20 | Blood of Yeshua |
| 2 Peter 2:3 | Judgment of false prophets and teachers |
| Jude 4 | Judgment of false believers |
| Revelation 9:15 | Four angels of one third world destruction |

| Revelation 13:8 | Names written in book of life (and Yeshua's sacrifice) |
| Revelation 17:8 | Names not written in book of life |

Because God had a predestined plan for the human race before the foundation of the earth, we can know that what happens around us is not by chance but by design. God gave us free will and set before us a series of spiritual and moral tests (**Deut. 30:15, 19**). He designed the outcome of those tests according to our responses.

What God created at the beginning of Genesis had in mind what happens at the end of Revelation. The end was planned from the beginning. This can be compared to a building contractor who would not start the construction until the entire plan was already designed by the architect. God's purpose for creation was already planned before He started the creation itself. The end product is determined by the original design.

There is a rabbinic saying (referring to the Sabbath) that goes, "What is last in deed is first in thought." Another rabbinic saying (about free will and predestination) goes, "All is foreseen, but free choice is given." God has a design from the beginning of time. What happens at the beginning of the Bible is a foundation for what will happen at the end of the Bible.

*Appendix Ten*
## Human and Glorified Appearances

Yeshua is revealed throughout the Bible from Genesis to Revelation as both God and man, (and the mediator between God and man—**1 Tim. 2:5**). At times Yeshua appears in a glorified form, emphasizing His divinity. At other times, He appears in an earthly form, emphasizing His humanity. (Yeshua is the Word of God that became flesh—**John 1:14**. So we could also call that earthly body—the body of flesh, or His "mundane" body.)

In the New Covenant Scriptures, the general pattern is that Yeshua appears in His earthly form in the gospels, and in His heavenly form in the book of Revelation. The only instance in which He is transformed into His glorified body in the gospels is on the Mount of Transfiguration (**Luke 9; Matt. 17**). He was glorified on the Mount of Transfiguration for the purpose of teaching us:

1. That He has a glorified, divine form
2. That is how we and He will look in the world to come
3. That we will be able to transition back and forth between those two forms at will whenever we desire

Yeshua also appears in both forms in the Hebrew Bible (Old Testament). A major appearance in an earthly body is found in **Genesis 18:** Along with the two angels who went on to destroy Sodom (**18:2** and **19:1**), He ate lunch and had a long discussion with Abraham about his son to be born and the judgment at hand. He also appeared in an earthly form at Peniel, where He wrestled all night with Jacob, as he was about to cross the border to reenter the Promised Land (**Gen. 32:2**). Another appearance (as the army commander with sword drawn) was to Joshua on the night before the battle of Jericho (**Josh. 5:13**).

Some examples of Yeshua's appearances in glorified form in the Hebrew Bible are the burning bush (**Exod. 3**), the crossing of the Red Sea (**Exod. 14**), on Mount Sinai (**Exod. 24**), on the King's throne exalted (**Isa. 6**), on the throne above the glory cloud and cherubim (**Ezek. 1:26**), brought before the Ancient of Days (**Dan. 7**) and as the man of fire in the book of Revelation (**Dan. 10:5**).

In the examples above in the Old Covenant, Yeshua appeared in an earthly form to people in the Land of Israel and in a glorified form to people outside the Land. The same is true for the New Covenant: His earthly appearances to the disciples were inside Israel, while His glorified appearance to John was in exile on the Isle of Patmos (**Rev. 1:9**).

While it is an oversimplification, there is a general pattern throughout Scriptures that the Son of God appeared in human form inside Israel and in glorified form outside the Land.[In Hebrew, the word for exile is *GALUT,* and the word for revelation is *HIT-GALUT.* The two words are from similar roots—*G-L-H* and *G-L-L.*]

This pattern—both in the New Covenant and the Old—that the divine appearances of the Messiah occur among the Gentile nations, while the human appearances of the Messiah occur within the Land of Israel, touches on the destiny of God for the Church and for Israel. The Church has held Yeshua's divinity, often missing the significance of His humanity. Israel has held the Messiah's humanity, often missing His divinity.

The Church has carried the Divine nature; Israel has carried the Davidic. In this generation, Israelis are coming to faith in Yeshua, and the Church is returning to her Jewish roots. The dual nature of the Son of God is being revealed in its fullness. (The Bride—of Israel and the Church—is taking up her dance as the "double camp" [**Song of Sol. 6:13**]; the Groom will return soon for the marriage [**Rev. 19:7**]. As Jacob and Esau—Jews and Arabs—are reconciled as the "double camp" [**Gen. 32:2**], the face of God, *Peniel* will be revealed.)

The reconciliation and the revelation go together. Within the reconciliation of Israel and the Church comes the complete revelation of Messiah Yeshua.

## *Appendix Eleven*
## Divine and Davidic

There is a development in the understanding of God's kingdom and of the nature of God throughout the Hebrew Scriptures. As the number of the people of God grew, so did the understanding of their relationship with God. Let's list a few of the significant stages of that historic development:

| | |
|---|---|
| To Noah | Family |
| To Abraham | Tribe |
| To Moses | Chosen People |
| To David | Israelite Kingdom |
| To Isaiah | Messianic Kingdom (prophesied) |

That development of the people of God continued into the New Covenant in three more stages:

| | |
|---|---|
| To Peter | Messianic Kingdom (revealed) |
| To Paul | International Church |
| To John | New Heavens and New Earth |

In the New Covenant, Scriptures there is a corresponding development in the understanding of who Yeshua is. It starts with the Davidic in the gospel of Matthew and progresses toward the Divine in the book of Revelation. The three parallel stages may be summarized as:

1.  Yeshua as king of Israel—Synoptic Gospels
2.  Yeshua as head of Church—Pauline Epistles
3.  Yeshua as angel of YHVH—Johanine Writings

The New Covenant starts in Matthew with the genealogy of Yeshua. This chapter is a bridge which connects the gospel events to the biblical history of Israel's kingdom. The emphasis is that Yeshua is the son of David. [**Note:** My friend, Dr. Michael Brown, pointed out the reason the genealogy is divided into periods of 14 (vv. 17-18). In Hebrew there are no vowels; therefore the equivalent of David is spelled: DVD. Each letter has a numerical value: D is 4; V is 6. David's name equals 4-6-4, totaling fourteen. The number fourteen emphasizes that Yeshua is David's son.]

God gave the government of planet earth to David (2 Sam. 7). If we don't understand the Davidic nature of Yeshua, we miss our dominion over this planet, the transformation of the kingdoms of the world (Rev. 11:15), the restoration of the kingdom to Israel (Acts 1:6), and the literal nature of the millennial kingdom. That's why the connection to David is so important.

If we miss the Divine nature of Yeshua, we miss our own created destiny to be human beings created in the image and likeness of God (**Gen. 1:26**). He has the fullness of God dwelling in Him in bodily form (**Col. 2:6**). As the people of God, we are destined to have the fullness of God dwelling in us as well (**Eph. 3:19**). The progression of the New Covenant Scriptures reveals Yeshua in stages from the Davidic to the Divine.

*Appendix Twelve*

**Scholarly Support**

*Messianic Theology and a Lost Judaism*

By Daniel C. Juster, Th. D.

Asher's book is a credible and significant contribution to the dialogue with Jews and Christians. *It restores a lost Judaism.* Generally, Messianic Jews are accused of having left the fold due to our unique theology, but we claim the deepest historical rooting for our Jewish theology! Our claim is that our movement is a resurrection of sorts and our theology is a return to an authentic Judaism that was unfairly precluded as Rabbinic Judaism developed over the centuries.

In the middle of the nineteenth century, E. W. Hengstenberg in Germany, wrote the classic *Christology of the Old Testament*. This large volume exhaustively covers every Hebrew text where the divine Messiah appeared in pre-incarnate form. Sometimes one gets the impression that Hengstenberg over pressed some texts to see Yeshua in them, but the volume remains an invaluable resource. Dr. Walter Kaiser, former Professor of Old Testament at Trinity Evangelical University, Deerfield, Illinois, and recently President of Gordon Conwell Divinity School, has published a volume updating Hengstenberg's work. In this book one will find very good scholarly support for Asher's writing.

The influence of Hengstenberg and Kaiser can be seen in my book *Jewish Roots* where I argued for the Angel/YHWH as an appearance of the pre-incarnate Messiah in my section on Yeshua's divinity. While my section is nowhere near comprehensive, it is indeed going in the very same direction as Asher.

More stunning are recent books by Jewish scholars on this issue. I will only name two. Alan Seigel in his very frequently quoted book, *Two Powers in Heaven* researched the idea of a plurality in the one God, and the sense of a lesser god who appears in the Bible and also is found in the inter-testament Jewish literature. It appears from Seigel's work that *the overly singular idea of God was not the only Jewish view in the first century.*

Daniel Boyarin is an esteemed Orthodox Jewish scholar and a professor at the University of California at Berkley. In his book *Borderlines,* Boyarin argues from a very full examination of the Bible and the inter-testament literature that *a plurality idea of the one true God was the majority view of first century Judaism.* The Angel/YHWH, the Word (Logos/Memra) and

Wisdom are identified together. Boyarin makes the claim that this figure is described as close to later creedal Christianity which describes the Son as a person (or Hypostasis) alongside the Father. Due to the Christian claim associating Yeshua with Logos, Wisdom and the Angel, Rabbinic Judaism turned away from this more ancient view.

Boyarin examines the post first century Jewish literature to show the evidence in Rabbinic Jewish texts of opposition to Christianity (and Messianic Judaism). These texts show a Rabbinic Judaism seeking to cleanse Judaism of these older ideas. While one sees the evidence of this attempt in the Talmud, the older view was hard to eliminate and still was popular among the ordinary people in the synagogues. Boyarin's book should be read to gain the full force of his argument, which I think cannot be refuted.

It is worthy to mention as well two prominent Christian scholars who have written extensively on the deity of Yeshua. Richard Bauckham of St. Andrews University in Scotland, in *God Crucified,* delivers a powerful volume showing that the claim of full deity for Yeshua is pervasive in the books of the New Covenant Scriptures. He is well versed in the ideas of God's uni-plural nature in first century Judaism. He makes the important claim that *the incarnation of God in Yeshua contradicts nothing in first century Judaism.* Why then was it rejected by the majority of Jewry? In Bauckham's view the majority of Jewish religious leaders simply could not embrace *the surprise* of the Incarnation. The issue was not the claim of plurality in God, but the Incarnation itself.

In addition, perhaps even more of a factor, the idea of a crucified Messiah was a scandal. Plurality was a common first century view but not the idea that the Logos/God could be fully incarnate in a human being of flesh and blood. While the Incarnation did not contradict anything in first century Jewry it was a surprise; too much of a surprise for Jewry. Therefore, after the first century, Rabbinic Judaism sought to embrace a singularity type monotheism that would make the theology of the New Covenant Scriptures seem heretical.

Larry Hurtado, now also of St. Andrews, in his many writings has argued that the devotional language of the New Covenant Scriptures is mostly binitarian (two-fold). Worship is constantly addressed to the Father and the Son, or the Father and Yeshua. This is an amazing development. (There is also but more rarely triune devotion.) This change of devotion is rooted in the early Messianic Jewish community and also in the binitarian passages in the Hebrew Scriptures that Asher so well describes. The Hebrew passages did not produce a clear binitarian devotion (although there were indications of devotion to Wisdom or Logos). However, after the incarnation, in the

New Covenant Scriptures, passages such as John 5 state explicitly that the Son is to be honored just as we honor the Father.

While views in accord with Messianic Jewish theology have not yet gained the dominant position in the world of theology, we live in a time where there is more scholarship supporting Messianic Jewish perspectives than ever before. Jewish scholars have written books declaring that the first century Jewish views included a uni-plural God as noted above. There are also Jewish scholars defending the legitimacy of the Messianic Jewish movement (Rabbi Cohn-Sherbuck, *Messianic Judaism*) and even defending the thesis that Yeshua rose from the dead (Orthodox Rabbi Pinchas Lapide in *The Resurrection of Jesus, a Jewish Perspective*).

There is much modern scholarship that supports the views expressed in Asher's book. However, God can also reveal these things to His children even without pursuing the scholarly books and journals!

# ABOUT THE AUTHOR
## *Asher Intrater*

Asher Intrater is director of ***Revive Israel*** Ministries and founder of Ahavat Yeshua Congregation in Jerusalem. He holds degrees from Harvard University, Baltimore Hebrew College, and Messiah Biblical Institute. He is the author of numerous books and tracts in Hebrew and English, including ***Covenant Relationships, What Does the Bible Really Say about the Land*** and ***From Iraq to Armageddon.***

In addition, Asher and the ***Revive Israel*** team publish weekly articles on the internet, translated into 10 languages around the world. These informative articles deal with current events in the Middle East, Bible teachings on end time prophecies, and updates on Messianic Jews and Arab Christians in Israel. Asher and his wife Betty have four children and live in the Jerusalem area.

For more information, or to sign up to receive the weekly updates, go to **www.reviveisrael.org**.

**Intermedia
Publishing Group**

*Publishing That Works For You*

Do you want to purchase bulk copies of *Who Ate Lunch with Abraham?* or buy another book for a friend? Get it now at www.imprbooks.com.

If you have a book that you would like to publish, contact Terry Whalin, Publisher, at Intermedia Publishing Group, (623) 337-8710 or email: twhalin@intermediapub.com or use the contact form at: www.intermediapub.com.